AGENCY LIM

G000144178

The Relaxed Holiday Cook

compiled by
Sarah Willes, Hattie Deards & Davina Mulford

Editors: Hattie Deards and Davina Mulford
Index compilation: Davina Mulford
Photography: Michelle Moradi www.michellemoradi.com
Food styling: Hattie Deards and Davina Mulford

First published in the United Kingdom in 2012 by
Blues Books
www.bluesagency.co.uk

ISBN 978–0–9573955–0–3

Contents

Foreword

by Prue Leith, CBE

The hallmark of a good cook is relaxed confidence. No one knows this better than Blues Agency who, for over thirty years, have supplied all manner of holiday cooks – from top chefs for the rich and famous to more modest cooks making hearty casseroles for hungry skiers.

Proceeds from this book will go towards supporting Blues In Schools, a life-changing project which gives children with behavioural difficulties the skills to cook.

With all-time favourites from the Blues band of cooks, as well as contributions from well-known cooks such as Josceline Dimbleby and Sally Clarke, the recipes in this book are easily achievable, satisfying to cook, and truly delicious to eat.

Introduction

For many people food is one of the most enjoyable elements of a holiday. It usually involves eating out in local pubs and restaurants, strolling around food shops and markets, and cooking in your holiday house or villa. However idyllic this sounds, we all know that sometimes the reality can be very different. You may have hungry teenagers and children moaning and groaning, or a group of friends and family lurking around the kitchen waiting for something delicious to appear miraculously.

The idea for *The Relaxed Holiday Cook* sprang from conversations with people who were going on holiday. They were worried about cooking for groups of friends and children, and the amount of endless planning, shopping and frantic preparation that was going to be involved in order to enjoy a meal together. At this point we realised that we could help.

For thirty-four years Blues Agency has been providing cooks to City corporations, private individuals, royal households and large families alike. Where could one find better cooks to provide real recipes? *The Relaxed Holiday Cook* shares the no-nonsense recipes that our cooks, past and present, have carried from job to job, enabling them to cook for small or large numbers with minimal fuss in holiday houses and villas across the globe.

This is our third book and, as with *Secret Kitchens*, we will be putting a percentage of every sale towards enabling Blues in Schools to continue, and keeping their kitchen well equipped: we run regular cookery classes for children with emotional, behavioural and special educational needs, and link them in with the national curriculum. Over the ten years that we have been running the project, we have seen the benefits of our work and have students going on to study hospitality and catering.

Cooking for friends and family should be enjoyable, sociable, affordable and fun, especially when you are on holiday. We hope that this book helps you achieve this.

Almost every recipe in the book is intended for four to six people, and is easy to double, triple or more. The book concentrates specifically on simple relaxed food, not smart fine dining. There is the occasional formal recipe for those times when you may want things to be a bit more special.

We have created three main holiday destination sections: British Seaside, the Mediterranean, and Mountains and Countryside. We have also included smaller sub-sections covering cakes, baking, marinades and breakfast ideas. We have organised the recipes according to where we feel they are most likely to be cooked, according to climate and availability of fresh ingredients. But it is up to you as the cook to choose whatever recipe you fancy, whatever the weather and wherever you are.

One final word of advice: delegate jobs to everyone around you. Get the kids podding beans and peeling potatoes, tell the adults to bone the fish and chop the meat, open a bottle of wine and enjoy the communal experience of cooking together.

We would like to thank all our cooks and contributors for our wealth of recipes. We would also like to thank Annabel Graham-Wood for her recipe testing and patient input into the book, and Michelle Moradi for her food photography – www.michellemoradi.com.

Huge thanks as well to Howard Webster for his creative input, Jeremy Lewis for his editorial expertise and advice, and The Choir Press and Miles Bailey for their advice and knowledge. Thank you also to John Bowditch for allowing us to use a holiday photograph taken in Scotland.

NB: Please note that we are using medium-sized free-range eggs for our recipes. These recipes have been tested with a fan-assisted oven, so please increase the temperature by 20°C if you are using a non-fan-assisted one. Rest assured: most ovens now are fan-assisted.

Sarah's Top 10 Holiday Tips

Preparation for the holiday and suggestions to keep things simple when you are there.

1. Avoid having to go shopping when you arrive at your holiday destination. Roughly plan the meals for a few days, buy your groceries on-line and have them delivered to where you are staying. Don't forget the less glamorous essentials such as bin liners, washing-up liquid, olive oil and sea salt.

2. Make a large jar of both vinaigrette dressing and pesto sauce the day before you leave. Pack into a cool bag on departure, and store in the holiday house fridge as a vital staple.

3. Curries and tomato-based casseroles can be made in advance and always freeze well. Perfect to defrost and take for the first night.

4. Cook a large ham early on in the holiday, and serve with baked potatoes and salad. Use the leftover ham throughout the week for lunches, sandwiches, pie fillings, soups, pasta sauces, etc.

5. Pizza dough freezes well and is useful for when you have lots of little people to feed at short notice.

6. Keep a vat of homemade tomato sauce in the fridge. Use to top pizzas, add to minced beef to make a quick bolognaise sauce, or use as a simple pasta sauce for children.

7. For those who love their puddings, keep crumble mixture in the freezer. Sprinkle the frozen crumble mixture over fruit for a quick and easy pudding.

8. Order a roll of puff pastry when you do your on-line shop. Convert it into a quick pudding by sprinkling ground almonds on the top, followed by sliced apples. Dot with butter, sprinkle with sugar, and bake in the oven. Or make cheese straws by spreading the pastry with English mustard and grated cheese, cut into fingers and bake in the oven.

9. Make breadcrumbs using any scraps of bread left over from breakfast. Use for fish and chips, chicken goujons, fish cakes, gratin toppings, scotch eggs and homemade burgers.

10. Roast a chicken in advance and keep it warm by wrapping in layers of foil. It will stay hot for at least 2 hours. Jacket potatoes will also stay hot wrapped in foil and put in a warming oven at a very low temperature. Great if you want to go to the pub before lunch and come back to a stress-free meal.

SARAH WILLES

The British Seaside

Let's be honest, British holidays by the sea can be a little temperamental weather-wise. One day we're revelling in the summer sunshine and making the most of the long days, the next day huge clouds descend and we're watching back-to-back films while rain pours down the gutters. For this reason we have a variety of recipes to cover all seasons, and all fluctuations in climate.

But despite all this, there is nothing better than renting a house by the sea and enjoying everything our country's coastline has to offer. Take the time to devour cream teas, eat seasonal asparagus and fish from our local waters. Explore the local pubs, go for cliff-top walks, dig in rock pools, breath in the salty fresh air and build up your appetite.

Smoked fish gratin

*This is quick, easy to prepare and can be made earlier in the evening,
ready to put in the oven just before everyone sits down.
Serve it with melba toast.*

Serves 6   Preparation time: 15 minutes   Cooking time: 15 minutes

- 1 bay leaf
- 3 parsley stalks
- 300g smoked haddock
- 1 x 400g tin of chopped tomatoes
- splash of wine
- 1 clove garlic, crushed
- 50g gruyere cheese, grated
- 50g parmesan cheese, grated
- 300ml double cream
- 2 handfuls fresh breadcrumbs
- sea salt and black pepper

1. Lightly butter 6 ramekins, and preheat the oven to 180°C/gas mark 4.
2. In a medium sized saucepan or frying pan, bring 750ml of water to a gentle boil. Add the bay leaf and parsley stalks. Gently slide the fish into the water, and simmer for 6–7 minutes, until just cooked. Allow to cool, remove the skin and bones and flake into chunks.
3. Cook the tomatoes with a good splash of wine and the crushed garlic until almost all the liquid has evaporated (about 15 minutes). Divide between the ramekins.
4. Mix the cooked haddock and three quarters of the cheese into the cream. Season with salt and pepper. Pile this on top of the tomato mixture in the ramekins.
5. Mix the remaining cheese with the breadcrumbs, and sprinkle over the top.
6. Cook in the oven for 10 minutes, or until golden and bubbling.

CAROLINE HARLE

Marinated kippers

Use Isle of Man or Scottish kippers if you can, or hunt down a local smoke house and get the finest kippers you can get hold of. Preparation time will be much quicker if you get filleted kippers.

Serves 4–6 as a starter   Preparation time: 20–40 minutes, dependent on the removal of bones   Marinating time: 6 hours

- 3 large kippers or 6 kipper fillets
- 1 medium red onion, thinly sliced
- 2 bay leaves
- 3 tbsp cider or white wine vinegar
- 6 tbsp olive oil
- 1 heaped tbsp sugar or to taste
- horseradish sauce to serve
- lemon wedges
- pinch of ground black pepper

1. Remove the bones first if you have whole kippers. Thinly slice the kipper fillets, and place in a shallow dish.
2. Mix together the onion, bay leaves, vinegar, olive oil, sugar and pepper.
3. Pour this over the sliced kippers and leave to marinate in the fridge for 6 hours, turning a few times.
4. Pile the kippers on each plate and serve with melba toast or buttered brown bread and horseradish sauce.

PAULINE WILLES

Crab and asparagus salad with chargrilled ciabatta

Serves 4 as a starter   Preparation time: 15 minutes   Cooking time: 20 minutes

- 200g parmesan
- 300g fresh white crabmeat
- 2 tbsp olive oil
- juice of ½ a lemon
- ½ red chilli, finely diced
- 12 spears of asparagus
- 1 clove garlic, cut in half
- 1 small loaf ciabatta
- sea salt and black pepper

1. Preheat the oven to 180°C. Line a baking sheet with baking or silicone paper.
2. Grate the parmesan and arrange into 4 piles on the baking sheet. Spread each pile out into a circle 8cm in diameter. Cook in the oven for 10–12 minutes until bubbling and golden brown. Watch out as these can burn easily. Allow to cool on a wire rack.
3. In a bowl, season the crab with salt and pepper and mix in the olive oil, lemon juice and the diced red chilli.
4. Trim the woody ends off the asparagus and blanch in a saucepan of boiling water for 3 minutes or until just cooked, and drain. Plunge into a bowl of iced water for 2 minutes (this helps keep the vibrant green colour) and drain again.
5. Heat a chargrill pan so that it is very hot. Slice the ciabatta into 2cm thick slices. Drizzle the slices of ciabatta with some extra oil on both sides and chargrill for 2 minutes on both sides. Rub the cut side of the garlic clove over the chargrilled slices of ciabatta and cool on a wire rack.
6. To serve, put a spoonful of the crab mixture, and a couple of asparagus spears on the plate. Prop the parmesan crisp up against the crab. Serve the chargrilled ciabatta on the side.

Helpful Hints:

❖ Use marsh samphire instead of asparagus if you can get hold of it.
❖ If you don't have a chargrill pan, the ciabatta can be toasted in a toaster or under a grill.

DAVINA MULFORD

Prawn and dill salad

Simple but delicious. Make sure you use the finest prawns you can get your hands on, and you won't be disappointed.

Serves 4–6 Preparation time: 10 minutes

- 1kg good quality large cooked prawns
- 5 sticks of celery
- ½ a red onion
- 1 bunch of dill
- 4 little gem lettuces
- 5 tbsp good quality mayonnaise, preferably homemade
- juice of 1 lemon
- 2–3 tbsp of extra virgin olive oil
- sea salt and black pepper

1. Remove the heads and peel and de-vein the prawns. Finely slice the celery, dice the red onion and finely chop the dill.
2. Cut off the bottom of the lettuces and remove the leaves. Wash the leaves and arrange on a large serving platter.
3. Mix the prawns with the dill, celery, red onion, mayonnaise and lemon juice, and season with salt and pepper.
4. Spoon the prawns onto the crispy lettuce leaves, spooning any remaining mayonnaise mixture over the salad leaves, and garnish with any leftover dill and a lemon wedge.
5. Finally, drizzle the salad with extra virgin olive oil and serve immediately.

Helpful Hints:

- ❖ Use langoustines if you are lucky enough to get hold of them.
- ❖ This is surprisingly filling so either serve as a starter for six or light lunch for four.
- ❖ Diana Horsford's homemade bread on p.70 goes well with this salad.

MIRANDA MARTIN

Brussel sprout, apple and walnut salad, p.7
Upside down beetroot tart, p.8

Brussel sprout, apple and walnut salad

An unusual winter salad. Surprisingly filling, so enjoy it as a light lunch.

Serves 4–6   Preparation time: 15 minutes   Cooking time: 5 minutes

- 400g brussel sprouts
- 100g mature cheddar cheese
- 1 large apple
- 2 tbsp olive oil + 1 tsp
- 50g walnuts
- 1 tsp cumin or caraway seeds
- A few thyme sprigs
- 1 lemon, juiced
- sea salt and black pepper

1. Peel the outer leaves off the sprouts, and finely slice them, discarding any hard base.
2. Grate the cheddar cheese. Peel and core the apple, and cut into fine matchsticks.
3. Heat a teaspoon of olive oil in a large non-stick frying pan, and gently toast the walnuts and cumin or caraway seeds. When lightly toasted, tip them into a salad bowl.
4. Heat the remaining two tablespoons of olive oil in the pan. Pull the thyme from the sprigs and add it to the pan along with the sprouts. Gently cook the sprouts until just tender. Add the juice of half a lemon.
5. Tip the tenderised spouts into the salad bowl, along with the walnuts, and add the apple and grated cheese. Gently mix together all the ingredients.
6. Season with salt and pepper, and add the remaining lemon juice to taste.

OLIVER GLADWIN

Upside down beetroot tart

Even the most steadfast of beetroot haters can't fail to give in to this tart. Serve for lunch with a green salad, or as part of a summer buffet.

Serves 4   Preparation time: 15 minutes   Cooking time: 1½ to 2 hours approx.

- 500g raw beetroot
- 75g butter
- 30g soft brown sugar
- 3 tbsp red wine vinegar
- 1 sprig of fresh thyme
- 1 pack of rolled puff pastry – approximately 320g
- 70g goats' cheese or feta cheese
- sea salt and black pepper

1. Preheat the oven to 180°C/gas mark 4.
2. Peel the beetroots and cut into quarters (if using baby beetroot, just cut in half).
3. Heat the butter in a frying pan with an ovenproof handle. When it is starting to gently bubble, add the beetroot pieces. Add the vinegar to the pan, and sprinkle over the brown sugar, shaking the pan and letting it melt into the butter and vinegar.
4. If you are using very soft stem thyme, place the thyme around the beetroot. If you are using thyme with a twiggy stem, remove the thyme leaves and scatter them over the beetroot. Season with salt and pepper.
5. Allow the pan to bubble gently for 5 minutes, then cover with foil and place in the oven for 1 hour to 1½ hours, or until the beetroot is soft. Make sure that the rounded side of the beetroot pieces are facing down in the pan, so that they look their best when you finally turn them out. There should be a syrup forming around the beetroot.
6. When soft, cover the beetroot with a sheet of ready-rolled puff pastry, tucking it well into the sides of the pan. Return to the oven and cook for a further 20 minutes, or until the pastry is golden brown and well puffed up.
7. Allow the pan to cool slightly before turning it upside down on to a plate, so that the beetroot is facing upwards. Sprinkle over a few fresh thyme leaves for colour and crumble over the goats' cheese or feta.

HATTIE DEARDS

Fish and potato chowder

*Nothing embodies seaside holidays more than fish soup.
Tuck in and savour the salty sweet combinations
of this chowder.*

Serves 6   Preparation time: 15 minutes   Cooking time: 20–25 minutes

- 750g cod, haddock or smoked haddock
- 6 rashers of smoked streaky bacon
- 1 tsp light olive oil
- 425ml fish stock or cooking liquor from simmering the fish
- 1 onion, finely chopped
- 800g raw potatoes, diced
- 2 carrots, diced
- 200g approximately of sweetcorn, tinned or on the cob
- 425ml milk
- pinch of paprika
- chopped parsley – optional
- sea salt and black pepper

1. Fill a medium pan with boiling salted water, and poach the fish gently in it for approximately 10 minutes, until the fish is only just done.
2. Remove the fish from the pan, and set aside. When it is cool enough to handle, remove any skin and bones, and cut into substantial chunks.
3. Cut the bacon into small squares and fry in a teaspoon of olive oil until crisp in a large non-stick saucepan. Add the fish stock or cooking liquor from simmering the fish, diced onion, carrots, sweetcorn and potatoes. Cook gently for 6 minutes, add the fish and cook for a further 2 minutes. Most importantly, do not let the potatoes over-cook. They should be only just cooked.
4. Add the milk, a pinch of paprika and a grind of black pepper. Heat through, then check the seasoning, and add sea salt to taste.
5. Stir through some finely chopped parsley, should you wish, before serving.

HATTIE DEARDS

Ginger fish with wok fried cabbage

Serves 4–6 Preparation time: 5 minutes Cooking time: 15 minutes

- 1 tbsp light olive oil/ground nut oil
- 1–2 large fillets per person of sea beam, red mullet or bass
- 1 red chilli, sliced in half and deseeded
- 1 clove of garlic, peeled
- 2-inch piece of ginger, peeled
- 6 tbsp light soy sauce
- 2 limes

1. Preheat oven to 180°C/gas mark 4.
2. Oil a rectangular oven tray. Line the fillets in a row, skin side down.
3. Finely chop the chilli, garlic and ginger, and sprinkle over the fish. Spoon over the soy sauce, and bake in the oven for 15 minutes.
4. Serve with wedges of lime, rice and wok-fried cabbage.

Wok-fried cabbage

Serves 4–6 Preparation time: 2 minutes   Cooking time: 4–6 minutes

- a large green cabbage
- 2 tbsp sesame oil
- ½ tbsp oyster sauce
- 5 tbsp light soy sauce

1. Halve the cabbage, remove the core and slice it thinly into ribbons.
2. Heat the oil in a wok or large frying pan. Add the cabbage, oyster sauce and soy sauce, and stir fry for approximately 4 to 6 minutes, until cooked.
3. Serve with the fish and rice.

Helpful Hints:

- ❖ For a nutty flavour, add toasted sesame seeds to the wok-fried cabbage at the end of the cooking process.

SARAH WILLES

Pasta with walnut and sun-dried tomato pesto, asparagus and fennel

Although I have used asparagus and fennel in this recipe, you can actually use whatever leftover vegetables you have in your fridge at the end of the holiday, making it a perfect last-night supper. Using walnuts in the pesto gives it a lovely 'earthy' flavour.

Serves 6   Preparation time: 15 minutes   Cooking time: 30 minutes

- 2 bulbs fennel
- 2 bunches asparagus
- 1 large bunch basil
- 80g sundried tomatoes
- 75g parmesan
- 2 fat cloves of garlic, peeled
- 40g walnuts
- 200ml olive oil + 3 tbsp
- 500g rigatoni
- sea salt and black pepper

1. Preheat the oven to 200°C/gas mark 6.
2. First of all, cut the fennel in half and then into small wedges. Lay the fennel wedges in a roasting tray, drizzle with 3 tablespoons of olive oil and season with salt and pepper. Cook in the oven for 20 minutes.
3. Cut the woody ends off the asparagus and cut each spear into 3 pieces. After the fennel has been cooking for 20 minutes, add the asparagus to the roasting tray and toss around with the fennel. Cook for a further 10 minutes.
4. In a food processor, whizz together the basil, sun-dried tomatoes, parmesan, garlic and walnuts, followed by the olive oil. Check the seasoning and add salt and pepper. You may need to add more olive oil if the pesto is too thick.
5. Cook the pasta in a large pan of salted boiling water until al dente. Drain the pasta and stir in the pesto, asparagus and fennel.
6. Serve with some parmesan shavings, chargrilled ciabatta and a green salad.

Helpful Hints:

- ❖ Don't worry if you don't have any walnuts, you can use any nuts – macadamia, pine nuts, blanched almonds, etc.
- ❖ I like to use the oil that the sun-dried tomatoes have been kept in for the pesto – this adds flavour and also saves waste.
- ❖ You can also use the pesto as a dip for crudités.

DAVINA MULFORD

Russian vegetable pie

Alexandra Galitzine was of Russian descent, and this is a family recipe of hers. She was a very dear friend of mine who spent many years cooking on yachts.

This pie has become a firm favourite in the Blues office, despite its somewhat unusual-sounding marriage of ingredients.

Serves 4–6   Preparation time: 20 minutes   Cooking time: 35–40 minutes

- 2 rolls of ready-made short crust pastry
- 30g butter
- 1 small head of white cabbage, sliced into thin shreds
- 1 large onion, halved and cut into semicircles
- 1 heaped tbsp of chopped dill
- 1 tbsp each of chopped tarragon and basil
- 250g mushrooms
- 4–5 hard-boiled eggs
- 125g cream cheese
- 1 egg, beaten
- sea salt and black pepper

1. Preheat the oven to 200°C/gas mark 6.
2. Roll out one roll of pastry and line a 9-inch pie dish. Roll out the other roll of pastry and using a small knife, cut it into a circle, one inch larger than the pie dish. Chill the lined pie dish and pastry disc in the fridge.
3. Slice the cabbage and onion and fry in a large sauté pan with half the butter for 10 minutes, until soft and lightly browned. Take off the heat, stir in the chopped herbs and season well with salt and pepper.
4. In another smaller pan, add the remaining butter and sauté the mushrooms lightly for 5 minutes, until cooked down.
5. Meanwhile, boil the eggs for 10 minutes. Drain out the water and set aside.
6. Take the pastry case and disc out of the fridge. Spread the cream cheese over the base of the pastry in the pie dish. Peel and slice the eggs, and arrange in a layer over the cream cheese.
7. Cover with the cabbage and onion mix. Make a final layer with the sautéed mushrooms and cover with the pastry disc. Press down, trim and flute the edges, and make a couple of short slashes through the top with a sharp knife.
8. Brush the top of the pie with the beaten egg and bake in the oven for 15 minutes, before turning the oven down to 180°C/gas mark 4 for a further 20–25 minutes, or until the crust is light brown.

Russian vegetable pie, p.12

Chicken, leek and anything-you-like pie

It's pretty difficult to make a pie inedible, but follow this basic recipe and you cannot go wrong. Use this as a base to add any leftovers you might have in the fridge, and you will have the perfect filling and a satisfying family pie. Let the creative in you take over.

Serves 6   Preparation time: 30 minutes   Cooking time: 25–30 minutes

- 500–700g raw chicken, cut into rough chunks
- 2–3 tbsp seasoned plain flour
- 75g butter
- 3 large leeks, trimmed and sliced
- 70–100g bacon or pancetta
- 200ml chicken stock
- 150ml milk
- 1 roll of puff or shortcrust pastry, approx 350g
- 1 egg
- sea salt and black pepper
- 200g asparagus, spinach, mushrooms or artichokes – or whatever additional vegetable you fancy

1. Preheat the oven to 200°C/gas mark 6.
2. Cut the chicken into rough chunks, toss with the seasoned flour and set aside in a large bowl. Slice the leeks into circles and cube the bacon or pancetta. Heat half the butter in large frying pan and sauté the leeks and bacon until softened. Tip into a bowl.
3. Heat the remaining butter in the same frying pan, and sauté the chicken pieces until golden and barely cooked. Tip the leeks back into the pan with the chicken, and gradually add the stock and milk, and allow it to bubble and thicken. You can do this in batches if the pan is not big enough. You should have a thickish sauce surrounding your chicken.
4. Meanwhile cook your vegetable of choice until just cooked. You can do this by pan frying, steaming or boiling – or simply adding any leftovers that need using up.
5. Pack the chicken and leek mixture into a large ovenproof pie dish. Add the additional vegetables, season with salt and pepper and cover with pastry, tucking it in around the edges and decorating it enticingly with any leftover pastry. Crack the egg into a small bowl, whisk it with a fork and brush over all the pastry.
6. Bake the pie in the oven for 25–30 minutes, or until golden brown and bubbling around the edges.

Helpful Hints:

❖ To make the pie richer and more sumptuous use cream instead of milk in the sauce.
❖ You can use left-over cold chicken, instead of raw, if you have it. Chop into rough chunks, and add 3 teaspoons of seasoned flour to the sautéing leeks, before adding the liquid.
❖ Don't hesitate to add any leftovers you have in the fridge. Tasty suggestions are chorizo, ham, cold sausages, peas, carrots, sweetcorn. Don't be tempted to add any leftover roast beef or lamb.
❖ Chop in any herbs you might like – parsley, tarragon, chervil or thyme would go well.

Kedgeree

Adapted from Jane Grigson's recipe, this kedgeree is a staple in our family, including children and babies. The beauty of this informal brunch/lunch/supper is that you can add and subtract ingredients as you wish. Personally, I like it brimming with fish and made with brown rice.

Serves 4   Preparation time: 10 minutes   Cook time: 30–40 minutes

- 500–650g smoked haddock, salmon, plain haddock, kippers or any mix of hearty fish that you like
- 2 bay leaves and any parsley stalks
- 2 tbsp olive oil
- 1 large onion, chopped
- 175g long-grain or brown rice, well rinsed
- 2–3 tsp curry powder
- 150g approx of cooked, peeled prawns
- Large bunch of parsley, chopped
- 3 eggs, hard boiled and chopped roughly
- 50g butter
- 1 lemon, juiced
- sea salt and black pepper

1. In a large wide pan or frying pan, bring 1 litre of water to a gentle boil. Add 2 bay leaves and some parsley stalks. Gently slide the fish into the water, and simmer for 6–7 minutes, until just cooked. Remove the fish from the water, and set aside on a plate, covering with tin foil to keep warm. Keep the water for cooking the rice.
2. Heat the olive oil in a large non-stick pan. Add the onions, and cook until they start to soften. Add the rice, and stir well. Add the curry powder, and cook for a further minute. Add approximately 600ml of the fish liquor (the water you used to cook the fish) to the rice, and allow it to cook steadily until the liquid has been absorbed and the rice is cooked, adding extra liquor if you need to.
3. Meanwhile, remove any skin and bones from the fish, and flake it into chunks. Add the fish to the rice along with the prawns, chopped parsley, egg and lemon juice to taste, and finally the butter. Stir thoroughly, but gently, so as not to break up the fish too much, and season with salt and pepper.
4. The kedgeree should be creamy and sumptuous, with a citrus tang. Add more butter and lemon juice if you feel the need.
5. Serve with a large bowl of steaming peas.

HATTIE DEARDS

Peter's "Squorkburgers", p.17

Peter's pork and squid burgers "Squorkburgers"

These burgers were inspired by my favourite Chinese dish of steamed minced pork and squid. I decided that the same combination would have to work as burgers, and here is the result. I love barbecuing these outside my beach hut on the Isle of Wight.

Serves 4   Preparation time: 10 minutes   Cooking time: 20–30 minutes

- 2 medium banana shallots, or 1 onion
- 2 spring onions
- 1 tbsp of oil
- 500g good quality minced pork
- 100g washed squid tube, finely chopped
- 1 tsp grated ginger
- large handful of finely chopped coriander
- pinch Chinese five spice
- sea salt and black pepper

1. Finely chop the spring onions and shallots or onion. Heat a tablespoon of oil in a frying pan, and sweat the onions until soft.
2. In a large bowl mix together the pork, finely chopped squid, ginger, chopped onions, coriander, Chinese five spice and the salt and pepper. Using a fork or your hands mix the whole lot together.
3. Form the mixture into 4 burgers, and barbecue, grill or fry until completely cooked through.
4. Serve as traditional burgers or with egg fried rice.

Helpful Hints:

❖ You can use fresh or frozen squid for this recipe. If none of you are keen on squid, just miss it out – the burgers still taste fantastic.

PETER MULFORD

Jerk chicken

Jerk chicken traditionally uses Scotch Bonnet chillies, but we have used normal chillies in this recipe, which should be easier to find.

Serves 4   Preparation time: 10 minutes, plus overnight marinating
Cooking time: 30–40 minutes

- 1½kg chicken pieces, thighs and drumsticks
- 1 large onion
- 2 red chillies, de-seeded
- 2 cloves garlic
- 50g root ginger, peeled
- 1tbsp runny honey
- 120ml white wine vinegar
- 120ml dark soy sauce
- 1tsp ground allspice
- 1tsp thyme leaves
- ½ tsp ground pepper
- sea salt and black pepper

1. To make the marinade, blitz the onion, chillies, garlic, ginger, honey, vinegar and soy sauce in a food processor until smooth. Pour into a bowl and add the allspice, thyme leaves and pepper.
2. Slash the skin of the chicken pieces with a sharp knife and add the pieces to the marinade, making sure that all the chicken is coated in the marinade.
3. Marinate in the fridge for a minimum of 2 hours, or preferably overnight.
4. Preheat the oven to 200°C/gas mark 6.
5. Lay the chicken pieces skin side up in a roasting dish, pour the remaining marinade over the chicken, and cook in the oven for 30–40 minutes.
6. Serve with potato wedges or rice and peas and a salad and season with salt and pepper if necessary.

ROSIE MCARTHY

Ham with champagne

This is a traditional Willes family recipe which we serve alongside the turkey on Christmas Day. Cook on the first night of your holiday and you will have leftover ham to use throughout the week for sandwiches, pie fillings and so on.

Serves 6, with enough left over for 2 more meals
Preparation time: 10 minutes   Cooking time: 1½ hours

- 2kg of smoked ham
- half a bottle of champagne, cider or prosecco
- 10 peppercorns
- 2 bay leaves
- 10 cloves
- 1 orange, cut into 4 pieces
- 500ml apple juice
- 500ml chicken or vegetable stock

1. Put the ham in a large pan of cold water and bring to the boil, then simmer for 3 minutes and pour away the water.
2. Wash out the pan and add all the ingredients with the ham and bring up to the boil. Simmer for roughly 1½ hours, allowing approximately 50 minutes per kilo.
3. To serve, remove the fat, slice the ham, arrange the slices on warmed plates. Pour over a little of the cooking liquid.

Helpful Hints:

❖ The ham can also be reheated in the cooking juices and served with parsley sauce or mustard sauce. Or serve it cold with a baked potato and the brussel sprout and apple salad, on page 7.

DOUGLAS WILLES

Cockle risotto

We go to Islay, on the west coast of Scotland, every summer with our two small children and friends. We always spend a couple of mornings raking cockles on the beach and enjoy eating them.

Serves 6   Preparation time: 30 minutes   Cooking time: 40 minutes

- 3kg cockles
- ½ bottle of white wine + a glassful
- 3 cloves garlic, peeled and crushed
- 3 tbsp olive oil
- 1 large onion or 5 banana shallots, finely chopped
- 500g arborio rice
- 125g butter, cubed
- 75g parmesan, grated
- 1 bunch flat-leaf parsley, chopped (keep the stalks)

1. Wash the cockles well in cold water, rubbing them against each other and changing the water at least 6 times. Place them in a colander to drain.
2. Add the white wine, garlic and parsley stalks to a small saucepan, and bring to the boil.
3. In another large casserole pan, heat 1 tablespoon of the oil and add the cockles. Add the hot wine and immediately place a lid on the pan. Check the cockles – after 3 minutes they should all be opened. Pour the cockles into a colander over a bowl for all the juices to drain off.
4. Go through the cockles, and put any that have come out of their shells into one bowl, and the ones still attached to their shells in another. Discard any that have not opened. Pass the cooking liquor through a fine sieve and pour back into a saucepan for the risotto.
5. Sweat the shallots in 2 tablespoons of olive oil. When cooked but not coloured, add the rice and season. Stir well, and when it is beginning to get sticky, add the final glassful of wine.
6. Carry on stirring, and add more of the cockle stock – ladle by ladle – once the last ladle has been absorbed by the rice.
7. When the rice has taken on a creamy consistency, but the rice still has quite a bite to it, add the butter and parmesan and stir well to emulsify. Then add the shell-less cockles and chopped parsley. Leave the risotto to sit for 5 minutes, in which time it will thicken a bit and the rice will become al dente.
8. Place a ladle of risotto into a soup bowl and garnish with the clams in their shells and some extra shavings of parmesan.

Helpful Hints:

❖ **Give the risotto a bit of punch with a squeeze of lemon and chilli oil over the top.**
❖ **Cook the cockles in batches if you can't find a pan big enough.**

EMILY WATKINS *ex-Blues cook and owner and chef of the Kingham Plough*

Chicken with tomatoes and honey

I first made this after a visit to a market in Morocco. I came home laden down with chicken and ripe tomatoes. I used the spices in the house and came up with this stew.

Serves 4–6   Preparation time: 15 minutes   Cooking time: 1½ hours

- 1 tbsp olive oil
- 1½ kg chicken thighs and drumsticks
- 200g chorizo sausage, chopped
- 1 onion, finely chopped
- 2 garlic cloves, crushed
- 2 tsp cinnamon
- ¼ tsp ginger
- pinch of saffron
- ½ kg very ripe tomatoes, skinned and cut into large pieces
- 2 tbsp fragrant honey
- knob of butter
- ½ bunch coriander, chopped
- sea salt and pepper

1. In a large casserole dish, brown the chicken pieces in the olive oil on a high heat. Once they have browned take them out of the pan and set aside.
2. Drain off any excess fat in the pan, add the chorizo, onions and garlic to the pan, and fry on a medium heat for a few minutes. Put the chicken pieces back in the pan, along with the spices and tomatoes, and season with salt and pepper.
3. Simmer on a very low heat for 1 hour 15 minutes with the lid on, until the meat is falling off the bone. Stir in the honey and cook for a further 15 minutes with the lid off.
4. To finish, stir in the knob of butter and garnish with the chopped coriander. Serve with spiced couscous and salad.

Helpful Hints:

❖ If you can't find any coriander, flat-leaf parsley also makes a nice garnish.
❖ You can also use 4 x 400g tins of plum tomatoes if you don't have the time or inclination to skin fresh tomatoes.

ROSIE MCARTHY

Rosemary-scented cod with tomato and caper vinaigrette

This recipe has been kindly donated by Leith's School of Food and Wine, *and comes from* Leith's *Simple Cookery, by Viv Pidgeon and Jenny Stringer, Bloomsbury, 2008*

Serves 4   Preparation time: 10 minutes   Cooking time: 15 minutes

- 4 x 170g boneless cod steaks
- 3 tbsp olive oil
- 4 sprigs rosemary
- 1 small red onion, very finely diced
- 6 tbsp good quality olive oil
- 2 tomatoes, peeled, deseeded and chopped
- 1 tbsp capers, drained and rinsed
- 1 tbsp lemon juice
- ½ tsp caster sugar (optional)
- sea salt and black pepper

1. Preheat the oven to 200°C/gas mark 6.
2. Pinbone the cod steaks if necessary but do not skin them. Season the cod skin with salt and pepper.
3. Heat the oil in a non-stick frying pan and add the cod steaks, skin side down, with the sprigs of rosemary. Fry for 2–3 minutes or until the skin is crisp.
4. Transfer the cod to a baking tray and bake in the oven for 8–10 minutes or until cooked. It should be opaque and firm.
5. Meanwhile, make the dressing: mix together all the ingredients in a bowl and whisk well. Leave to infuse while the fish continues to cook.
6. To serve, lay the fish on a plate, and spoon the dressing around the outside. Garnish with a few rosemary leaves.

Helpful Hints:

❖ Serve with boiled new potatoes with chopped mint, and steamed courgettes.

LEITH'S SCHOOL OF FOOD AND WINE

Rosemary-scented cod with tomato and caper and vinaigrette, p.22

Oxtail with cider, prunes and beans

Josceline Dimbleby's recipes are a delight to the home cook: they always work, and they are always delicious. This recipe is taken from Orchards in the Oasis, Quadrille, 2010.
I was thrilled to discover that such a cheap cut of meat produced a dish so rich in flavour, and delighted to find that it tasted even better if made conveniently ahead and reheated the following day. Serve with mashed potato, which is lovely with the juices, and a green salad.

Serves 6   Preparation time: 15 minutes   Cook time: 3½–4 hours

- 3 large onions
- 2 tbsp sunflower oil or groundnut oil
- 1kg oxtail pieces
- 100g pitted prunes
- 450ml dry cider
- zest and juice of 1 orange
- 1 heaped tsp juniper berries
- 4 large cloves of garlic
- 1 x 400g tin of chopped tomatoes
- 1 x 400g tin of haricot beans, drained
- 10 sage leaves
- sea salt and black pepper

1. Preheat the oven to 240°C/gas mark 9.
2. Peel and slice the onions into semicircles.
3. Heat the oil in a large frying pan, and fry the oxtail pieces, in batches, until well browned all over. Transfer the meat to a large casserole dish with a slotted spoon.
4. Fry the onions in the same pan until soft, and then add them to the casserole with the oxtail.
5. Cut the prunes in half and add them to the casserole with the cider, grated orange rind and juice and the juniper berries. Season with salt and plenty of freshly ground pepper, and put the lid on.
6. Cook the casserole in the oven on the centre shelf for 20 minutes until the liquid is bubbling. Then lower the oven setting to 140°C/gas mark 1, and cook for a further 2½ hours, until the meat is very soft and starting to come away from the bones.
7. Peel the garlic, slicing the cloves thinly crossways, and add to the casserole with the chopped tomatoes, haricot beans and whole sage leaves. Return to the oven for 45 minutes. Leave until cold and then refrigerate or keep in a cold larder until the next day.
8. The next day spoon off the solidified fat from the top of the stew, put the lid back on and reheat in the oven at 200°C/gas mark 6, until bubbling. Adjust the seasoning as necessary.

JOSCELINE DIMBLEBY *Orchards in the Oasis*, Quadrille, 2010

Seven-hour leg of lamb with garlic and anchovies

Another dish you can assemble in minutes and simply forget about. Keep things simple and serve with baked potatoes and green salad, or a ratatouille

You will need a large ovenproof dish, big enough to hold the leg of lamb snugly with a lid on.

Serves 6   Preparation time: 20 minutes   Cooking time: 7 hours

- 1 x 1¾–2kg leg of lamb
- 5 anchovy fillets
- 3 large cloves garlic, peeled and quartered
- 1 tbsp olive oil
- 200g smoked streaky bacon
- 3 x sprigs each of rosemary, thyme and parsley
- 250ml chicken stock
- 250ml white wine
- sea salt and black pepper

1. Preheat the oven to 120°C/gas mark 1.
2. Pat the anchovy fillets free of excess oil and cut each one into 3 pieces. With a sharp knife, make 12 incisions deep in the meat on both sides of the leg of lamb. Force one piece of anchovy and one piece of garlic into each incision. Season the leg of lamb with salt and pepper.
3. Heat the olive oil in a large frying pan and fry the leg of lamb on both sides until it is golden brown. Remove the lamb and place in the ovenproof dish or casserole. Chop the bacon into 1 inch pieces and fry for 2 minutes. Add the bacon to the oven dish with the lamb, then add the herbs, chicken stock and wine. Put the lid on, stand the dish on a baking tray and place in the oven.
4. After 7 hours, take the dish out of the oven. Lift out the lamb and gently carve the meat (it will be very tender and will break up). Arrange on a large serving plate and pour over some of the juices. Serve the remaining juices in a jug so people can help themselves.

ZINNIA SWANZY

Fillet steak with aubergine, tomato and basil compote

This recipe is taken from Rachel Green's *Chatsworth Cookery Book, Green Shoots, 2007. Rachel has years of experience as a chef, outside caterer, demonstrator and food campaigner. She is a passionate and committed ambassador of British produce, and has been demonstrating at Chatsworth for many years.*

Serves 4   Preparation time: 10 minutes   Cooking time: 25 minutes

- 50ml olive oil
- 2 aubergines, cut into 1cm cubes
- 400g cherry tomatoes
- 2 cloves garlic, finely chopped or crushed
- 2 tsp thyme leaves
- 2 tbsp balsamic vinegar
- small bunch basil
- 1 tbsp vegetable or rapeseed oil
- 4 x 200g fillet steaks
- sea salt and black pepper

1. First make the compote. Heat the olive oil in a large sauté pan, add the aubergine and cook for 5–10 minutes until golden brown. Add the tomatoes and cook for a further 5–10 minutes until the tomatoes have split and softened. Add the garlic and thyme and cook for a further 2 minutes, before adding the balsamic vinegar.
2. Bubble until the liquid has reduced and the compote is thick. Roughly tear in the basil leaves, season well and leave to cool.
3. Heat a heavy-based griddle or frying pan until smoking. Brush the steaks with the oil and season well with salt and pepper.
4. Cook the steaks on the hot griddle for 2–3 minutes each side for rare steaks, or 4 minutes each side for medium. Remove the steaks from the pan and leave to rest for a couple of minutes before serving with a spoonful of the compote. These are best served with a green salad, and chips or new potatoes.

Helpful Hints:

❖ Fillet steak is very smart and expensive, but often other cuts are just as tasty and more economical. Buy yourself sirloin, T-bone or rib-eye steaks, and ask your butcher for cooking times depending on their weight.

❖ The compote can be prepared 24 hours in advance, and is best served at room temperature.

RACHEL GREEN

Crunchy raspberry ripple ice cream

Who wants to spend hours making ice cream when you're on holiday? This is the perfect compromise, filled with the tantalizing crunch of meringue.

Serves 4–6   Preparation time: 25 minutes   Freezing time: approximately 4 hours

- 350g raspberries, fresh or frozen, or 200g raspberry coulis
- 3 eggs
- 100g caster sugar
- 284ml double cream or crème fraiche
- 3 large meringue shells, broken into large chunks

1. Line a 1 litre loaf tin with cling film.
2. Puree the raspberries, and pass them through a sieve, discarding the seeds. You will not need to do this if you are using raspberry coulis.
3. Whisk together the eggs and sugar in a bowl over a pan of barely simmering water until thick and doubled in volume. Allow to cool slightly.
4. Whip the cream in a separate bowl until just thick, and gently fold in the egg mixture until completely combined.
5. Trickle some raspberry coulis in a zigzag pattern on the bottom of the loaf tin. Follow with a layer of the egg and cream mixture, and then sprinkle some chunks of meringues onto it. Repeat with layers of coulis, cream mixture and meringue.
6. Cover with cling film and place in the freezer for a minimum of 4 hours. Remove the cling film, turn the tin upside down on to a plate, ease the ice cream loaf out of the tin. Cut into slices and serve with more coulis and extra raspberries if wanted.

Helpful Hints:
- ❖ Don't hesitate to use shop-bought raspberry coulis and meringues – it makes little difference to the finished product.
- ❖ This pudding can be kept in the freezer for up to a month.
- ❖ If you are using thick crème fraiche, instead of cream, don't try to whip it; just fold it gently into the egg and sugar mixture.

VICKY POWER

Vicky's crunchy raspberry ripple ice-cream, p.27
Tangerine and ricotta squares, p.29

Tangerine ricotta squares

These combine my two loves: cheese and lemon cake. These squares are perfect served after dinner with coffee, for those who have any room left for something sweet.

Serves 6   Preparation time: 15 minutes   Cooking time: 35–40 minutes

- 250g ground almonds
- zest of 6 tangerines and 1 lemon
- 225g butter
- 250g caster sugar
- 6 eggs, separated
- 300g ricotta cheese
- Juice of 2 tangerines and 1 lemon

1. Preheat the oven to 160°C/gas mark 3.
2. Combine the ground almonds and fruit zest.
3. In a bowl or food processor, beat the butter and sugar until creamy. Add the egg yolks one by one, and then the almond and zest mixture.
4. Put the ricotta in a bowl and beat in the fruit juice. In a separate bowl whisk the egg whites until firm, and then fold in the almond mixture. Finally stir in the ricotta.
5. Pour the mixture into a roasting dish lined with baking paper and bake in the oven for 35–40 minutes, until golden.
6. Once cooked, allow to cool for 10 minutes and then turn out onto a wire rack to cool completely. Cut into squares.

Helpful Hints:
- ❖ If you can't find tangerines, use clementines, satsumas or oranges.
- ❖ The squares store well in a cake tin, remaining moist for a good few days.

JAMES NATHAN

Apple and cinnamon French toast tarte tatin

You will need a 9–10 inch/23–26cm tarte tatin pan for this recipe, or an ovenproof frying pan with a metal handle.

Serves 4–6   Preparation time: 10 minutes   Cooking time: 30 minutes

- 3 apples
- 55g butter
- 55g soft brown sugar
- 1 tbsp ground cinnamon
- 2 eggs
- 3 tbsp caster sugar
- 300ml single cream
- 5 slices white bread, crusts on
- knob of butter

1. Pre-heat the oven to 190°C/gas mark 5. Peel, quarter, core and slice the apples.
2. Melt the butter in a shallow frying pan, and add the brown sugar and apple slices. Cook on a medium heat until the sugar dissolves and the apples begin to soften, then turn up the heat to evaporate some of the juice. Stir in the ground cinnamon, and set aside.
3. Beat the eggs with the caster sugar and cream. Dip the bread slices into the mixture and allow them to soak it up. Lay the bread slices over the apples, tearing and patching to fit.
4. Pour over any remaining custard and dot with butter. Bake in the oven for 30 minutes, until puffy and golden brown. Take out of the oven and leave for 5 minutes to cool slightly, before inverting onto a serving plate.
5. Serve while still warm with cream or praline ice cream.

Praline ice cream – turn your vanilla ice cream into something special ...

A handful of almonds (with their skin on) and 2 tablespoons of caster sugar:

Heat the almonds and caster sugar in a pan and cook until the sugar has dissolved and caramelized to a golden brown. Don't stir at any point. Pour the mixture on to baking paper and cool. Break up praline in a processor or with a rolling pin. Mix with your vanilla ice cream, or sprinkle over the top.

PAULINE WILLES

Warm chocolate mousse

A cross between a chocolate soufflé and a chocolate fondant, this pudding needs to be taken from the oven to the table fairly promptly. If your holiday house has no weighing scales, just guess the quantities – it never goes wrong.

Serves 6 Preparation time: 15 minutes + 1 hour chilling
Cooking time: 10–12 minutes

- 35g unsalted butter
- 125g dark chocolate
- 1 tbsp of strong espresso (can be substituted with liquor or vanilla essence)
- 3 eggs, separated
- 40g caster sugar

1. Melt the butter, chocolate and espresso in a bowl suspended over a simmering pan of water.
2. Once melted, remove and cool for 15 minutes before mixing in the egg yolks.
3. Whisk the egg whites while gradually adding the sugar until stiff peaks are formed.
4. Using a large metal spoon fold the egg whites into the chocolate mixture.
5. Pour the mix into ramekins and chill in the fridge for at least an hour.
6. Preheat the oven to 180°C/gas mark 4, and bake the mousses for 10–12 minutes.
7. Place the ramekins on to small plates, and serve immediately with a dusting of icing sugar, and a dollop of thick clotted cream or crème fraiche on top.

LOUISA MACFARLANE

Apple pie ice cream

Created at my home in Dorset, this is a favourite with all my family and friends.

Serves 4-6   Preparation time: 5 minutes   Cooking time: 20 minutes
Freezing time: 4 hours minimum

- 2 cooking apples
- 3 tbsp water
- 2 tsp cinnamon
- 1 large pinch ground cloves
- 2 heaped tbsp caster sugar + 2 tsp caster sugar
- 250ml double cream
- 500g natural yoghurt
- 1 sheet of shop bought puff pastry

1. Peel, core and quarter the apples. Place the apple pieces into a pan with the water, 1 tsp of cinnamon, ground cloves and 2 tablespoons of sugar. Cook the apples over a low heat until soft, approximately 10 minutes, and mash them with a fork or masher. Set aside to cool.
2. Whip the cream until thick, and fold into the apple mixture along with the yoghurt.
3. Pour the mixture into a Tupperware or plastic container, and place in the freezer for at least 4 hours, intermittently stirring the mixture 2 or 3 times. Alternatively you could use an ice cream maker.
4. When you are getting ready to serve your ice cream, preheat the oven to 180°C/gas mark 4. Roll out the puff pastry if you need to (it may already be in a sheet) and place it on a non-stick baking tray. Sprinkle over the remaining teaspoon of cinnamon and 2 teaspoons of sugar.
5. Cut the pastry into 8 cm squares, and cook in the oven for 10 minutes, until risen and golden.
6. Spoon the ice cream into bowls and place the hot squares of pastry on top, and serve immediately.

Helpful Hints:

❖ Delight in the hot and cold extremes, and serve with warm fudge sauce. You can make this with equal measures of butter, cream and soft brown sugar. Place all the ingredients in a small pan and melt together, allowing the sauce to bubble.
❖ Another pleasing accompaniment is peeled quarters of apple, lightly fried in a little butter.

SARAH WILLES

Davina Allen's panzanella, p.40
Sardine escabeche, p.48

The
Mediterranean

The thought of a holiday in the Mediterranean can be enough to keep us going through the dark winter months, and there are many reasons why. Crystal clear waters to swim in, bright colours, sunshine, local food markets, sea food, copious jugs of wine, siestas. The list goes on.

The Mediterranean, in the spring and summer months, can be a very hot place to be. We have put together a collection of recipes for this section that involve minimal cooking time, so you can keep well away from hot ovens and use the barbecue as much as possible.

Make the most of the amazing produce on hand, and you will find that the food will need very little tinkering with.

Charentais melon, goat's cheese and saucisson salad

*On an overcast winter's day in the office I concocted this salad
while daydreaming wistfully about holidays in the sun.
Amazingly the combination of ingredients worked
really well. Try this for yourself.*

Serves 4-6   Preparation time: 10 minutes

- 200g mange tout
- 1 charentais melon
- 200g saucisson sec
- 3 spring onions
- 2 large handfuls of rocket
- extra virgin olive oil and balsamic vinegar
- 200g goat's cheese
- sea salt and black pepper

1. Blanch the mange tout in a pan of salted boiling water for just 2 minutes, then drain and run under cold water to keep the vibrant green colour.
2. Cut the melon into 1cm chunks and slice the saucisson and spring onions.
3. Combine the melon, rocket, spring onions and saucisson in a bowl. Dress with salt, pepper, olive oil and balsamic vinegar, and mix all the ingredients together well. Top with crumbled goat's cheese.

Helpful Hints:

❖ If you can't get hold of saucisson, cured chorizo sausage works just as well.
❖ Curly endive lettuce is a good substitution for rocket.
❖ You may also wish to use a feta cheese instead of goat's cheese.

DAVINA MULFORD

Chilled tomato and chorizo soup

I spent a summer working for a family in the Hamptons, USA, and this Mediterranean-style soup was always popular with guests.

Serves 6 people   Preparation time: 15 minutes   Cooking time: 20 minutes

- 4 tbsp olive oil
- 2 onions, chopped
- 2 sticks celery, chopped
- 2 cloves garlic, crushed
- 300g chorizo, diced roughly
- 1 tsp smoked sweet paprika
- 2 sprigs thyme (leaves removed)
- 12 tomatoes on the vine, skinned and chopped
- 1 litre of vegetable stock
- a squeeze of lemon
- salt and pepper

1. Heat the olive oil in a large heavy-bottomed pan. Add the onion and celery, and sweat for about 5 minutes or until soft. Add the garlic, chorizo, paprika and thyme leaves, and cook for another 5 minutes.
2. Add the skinned tomatoes and stock and cook gently for 10 minutes.
3. Remove from the heat and blend using a hand blender or food processor. Check seasoning, adding salt, pepper and lemon juice to taste.
4. Serve chilled.

HELPFUL HINTS:

❖ Add colour to the soup with torn up basil leaves. Sprinkle over the soup just before serving.

EMMA TINNE

Nectarine, mozzarella and rocket salad with sweet chilli and lime dressing

This salad is punchy, invigorating and spicy. Serve and eat it quickly, and watch it disappear off every plate.

Serves 4–6   Preparation time: 10 minutes

- 100ml of sweet chilli sauce
- 50ml of fresh lime juice and zest of 1 lime
- 50ml of mild olive oil
- 3 ripe nectarines
- 2 balls of the best mozzarella you can buy (if in Italy buy burratta instead)
- 1 large handful of fresh mint
- 1 bag of freshly washed rocket
- sea salt and black pepper

1. Whisk together the sweet chilli sauce, lime juice and zest, and the olive oil for the dressing.
2. Wash the nectarines and cut each one into 8 segments.
3. Tear up the mozzarella and tear up the mint leaves.
4. Put the rocket into a large bowl or platter. Scatter over the nectarines, mozzarella and mint.
5. Drizzle the dressing over the top and season with salt and pepper.
6. Serve immediately.

JO PRESTON

Fennel and blood orange salad, p.39

Nectarine, mozzarella and rocket salad with sweet chilli and lime dressing, p.37

Butterbean salad with salsa verde dressing, p.42

38

Fennel and blood orange salad

Another quick, easy and healthy salad to have for lunch when the sun is shining. A cold glass of rosé wine is the perfect accompaniment.

Serves 4   Preparation time: 5–10 minutes

- 4 blood oranges
- 2 bulbs of fennel
- 100g manchego cheese or any other hard cheese
- 3 tbsp good quality olive oil
- 2 tbsp freshly squeezed orange juice
- 1 large handful rocket
- sea salt and black pepper

1. Peel the oranges and cut them into thin segments. Thinly slice the fennel and the cheese.
2. Make a dressing out of the olive oil, orange juice, salt and pepper.
3. Arrange the rocket, oranges and fennel on a plate and top with the cheese. Sprinkle with the dressing and serve.

BLUES

Darina Allen's panzanella

This recipe is taken from Darina Allen's Easy Entertaining, *Kyle Cathie, 2005. Darina owns the world-famous Ballymaloe cookery school in Ireland. We have a long-standing association with Ballymaloe, and visit the school each term to meet the students.*

Serves 4-6 Preparation time: 15 minutes

- 700g very ripe tomatoes
- 1 large red onion, sliced
- 450g 2-day old country bread, such as sourdough
- 125ml extra virgin olive oil
- 2 tbsp red wine vinegar or lemon juice
- 1 garlic clove, crushed or grated
- 1 tsp sugar, optional
- large bunch of basil, roughly torn
- slivers of parmesan cheese – optional
- sea salt and black pepper

1. Cut the tomatoes into chunks. Place them in a colander and sprinkle with salt, setting them aside to drain. Slice the onions, and set aside. Tear the bread up into rough chunks.
2. Mix together the olive oil, vinegar or lemon juice and garlic in a large salad bowl. Add the drained tomatoes, bread and onions. Season with salt and pepper, and sugar if you wish, and tear in the basil. Gently toss all the ingredients together. Taste and adjust the seasoning if you need to, and add parmesan shavings if you want.

Helpful Hints:

❖ Delicious served with peppery rocket leaves.

DARINA ALLEN

Duck and watermelon salad

Serves 4–6   Preparation time: 15 minutes   Cooking time: 2 hours

- 1 duck for roasting
- 100g roasted cashew nuts
- 6 spring onions
- small bunch mint
- ½ a chilled watermelon
- juice of 2 limes
- caster sugar to taste
- 1–2 tbsp light soy sauce
- 250g bean sprouts
- sea salt

1. Preheat the oven to 200°C/gas mark 6.
2. Prick the skin of the duck with a fork and rub the bird with salt. Roast it in the oven for an hour, basting occasionally.
3. Turn the oven down to 150°C/gas mark 2 and cook the duck for a further half an hour, before then turning up the heat to 200°C/gas mark 6 again for the last half an hour. Set aside.
4. Meanwhile, dry roast the cashew nuts in the oven or a dry frying pan. When lightly toasted, chop them roughly. Slice the spring onions, roughly chop the mint, and cut the watermelon into 2½ cm cubes. Add all the ingredients to a large salad bowl.
5. In a separate bowl, mix together the lime juice with a little sugar to taste, and add the soy sauce.
6. Just before serving, shred the hot duck, keeping the crispy skin. Add it to the salad bowl, along with the other ingredients and bean sprouts. Quickly add the dressing and serve immediately.

Helpful Hints:
- ❖ If you have trouble getting hold of bean sprouts, sliced chicory works just as well.

SARAH WILLES

Butterbean salad with salsa verde dressing

Serve either as a side dish, or as a main course with the Sicilian tuna ceviche on page 47.

Serves 4–6   Preparation time: 5 minutes

- 1 bunch flat-leaf parsley
- 1 bunch mint
- 150ml olive oil
- 1 clove garlic
- 1 tsp Dijon mustard
- 2 x tbsp capers
- juice of ½ a lemon
- 3 x 400g tins of butterbeans, rinsed and drained
- 200g sunblushed tomatoes
- ½ red onion, finely diced
- ½ cucumber, de-seeded and sliced
- sea salt and black pepper

1. To make the salsa verde, whizz together the parsley, mint, olive oil, garlic, mustard, capers and lemon juice in a food processor.
2. In a large bowl, mix the salsa verde with the butterbeans, tomatoes, cucumber and red onion. Season with salt and pepper, and serve.

DAVINA MULFORD

Sea Club salad

The Sea Club in Cala Ratjada, Mallorca, has been a regular place of employment and holidaying for Blues cooks and clients over the years. This salad slowly took shape over the years, although the original was created by Nora Cumberledge, founder of the Sea Club.

It's filling and economical, not to mention delicious.

Serves 6 people   Preparation time: 10 minutes   Cooking time: 30–40 minutes

- 275g long or short grain brown rice
- 1/3 to 1/2 white cabbage
- 85g dried apricots, chopped into small pieces
- 150g hazelnuts, roughly chopped and toasted
- 3 tbsp olive oil
- 3–4 tsp curry powder
- 2 tbsp mango chutney
- juice of half a lemon, to taste
- handful of chopped parsley
- sea salt and black pepper

1. Rinse the rice in a sieve and boil it in salted water for 30 minutes, or until cooked. Drain and set aside.
2. Finely slice the cabbage, so that it is in thin ribbons, and tip it into a large mixing bowl. Add the chopped apricots, toasted hazelnuts and the rice.
3. Heat the olive oil in a small pan and gently fry off the curry powder for a minute. Add the mango chutney, swirl it around and tip it over the salad. Squeeze over the juice of half a lemon, add the chopped parsley and give the salad a really good stir.
4. Season with salt and pepper.

Helpful Hints:
- ❖ This salad is the perfect vehicle for using up any stray vegetables that might be lurking in your fridge. Add celery, slices of apple, green beans – don't hold back.
- ❖ You can substitute dried apricots for fresh ones, sultanas or dates.
- ❖ If you have any leftover meat, such as chicken or lamb, add it to your salad.

NORA CUMBERLEDGE

Goat's cheese and sun-dried
tomato frittata, p.45

Kali's quinoa tabbouleh, p.46

Goat's cheese and sun-dried tomato frittata

Another vibrant recipe taken from Darina Allen's Easy Entertaining, Kyle Cathie, 2005. This frittata is colourful and inviting.

Serves 6–8   Preparation time: 10 minutes   Cooking time: 15–20 minutes

- 8 large free-range eggs
- a large handful of chopped parsley
- a handful of chopped basil and thyme
- 110g chorizo, cut into small chunks
- 40g grated parmesan
- 300g sun-dried or sun-blushed tomatoes
- 25g butter
- 110g goat's cheese
- sea salt and black pepper

1. Whisk the eggs together in a large bowl. Add the chopped herbs, chorizo and the parmesan cheese, and stir it all together thoroughly.
2. Add the tomatoes, cutting any particularly large ones in half, and stir gently. Season the mixture well with salt and pepper.
3. Add the butter to a large non-stick frying pan. When it starts to gently bubble, add the egg mixture to the pan, and turn the heat right down. Cut the goat's cheese into walnut-sized chunks, and scatter them over the top of the egg mixture.
4. Cook the frittata extremely slowly for around 15 minutes – the underneath should start to set, but you do not want it to burn.
5. When the bottom is set and the top is still runny, turn the grill onto a medium to low heat. Place the frying pan under the grill and cook for a few minutes, until the egg has fully set and the surface is very slightly browned.
6. When the frittata is cooked, slide it on to a plate, and serve it warm with a large green salad.

DARINA ALLEN

Kali's quinoa tabbouleh

Tabbouleh, but just a little bit different.

Serves 4–6   Preparation time: 25–30 minutes

- 200g quinoa
- Juice of 2 lemons
- 2 tbsp olive oil
- 1 cucumber, cut in half lengthways and seeds removed
- 2 small red onions, finely chopped
- large bunch parsley
- large bunch mint
- sea salt and black pepper

1. Boil the quinoa in enough stock or water to cover it well for 20–25 minutes, until just cooked. Drain and tip into a large mixing bowl.
2. Juice the lemons and pour the juice over the warm quinoa, add the olive oil and mix well. Halve the cucumber lengthways and scoop out the seeds with a teaspoon, then chop the cucumber into cubes. Add it to the quinoa along with the chopped onions.
3. Chop the parsley and mint, either by hand or in a food processor, and stir into the quinoa, and season to taste with salt and pepper.

KALI HAMM

Sicilian tuna ceviche

I had this dish in a restaurant on the Aolean island of Panarea, off the coast of Sicily. It is a simple recipe, but full of fantastic flavours, and makes a great starter. Use the freshest tuna you can buy.

Serves 4–6 as a starter   Preparation time: 15 minutes

- 400g fresh tuna, cut into 1cm cubes
- 3 tbsp capers
- 2 lemons, juiced
- ½ red onion, finely sliced
- 1 medium ciabatta loaf, cut into diagonal slices
- 4–5 tbsp extra virgin olive oil
- 1 clove of garlic
- 2 handfuls of rocket
- 10 mint leaves, finely shredded
- sea salt and black pepper

1. Mix together the tuna, capers, lemon juice and red onion in a large bowl, and leave to marinate and 'cook' for 10 minutes.
2. Heat a griddle pan, or frying pan, to a very high heat. Drizzle the slices of ciabatta bread with 2–3 tablespoons of the olive oil, and chargrill on both sides. Cut the garlic clove in half, and rub the cut side over the toasted ciabatta slices, and leave to cool on a wire rack.
3. Arrange the rocket on a serving dish, and spoon over the tuna mixture. Season with extra pepper, drizzle over the remaining olive oil, and scatter over the mint leaves.

Helpful Hints:
❖ If you have a barbecue going, use this to chargrill the ciabatta instead of a griddle pan.

DAVINA MULFORD

Sardine escabeche

This is best made the day before and left in the fridge for 24 hours to marinate. Serve as a starter with some crusty bread and unsalted butter.

Serves 4–6   Preparation time: 20 minutes   Cooking time: 20 minutes

- 12 sardines, gutted, scaled, with heads removed
- 50g plain flour, seasoned with salt and pepper
- 250ml good quality olive oil
- 150ml red wine vinegar
- 2 onions, sliced
- ½ tsp dried chilli flakes
- 1 orange, zested
- 2 fresh bay leaves
- 1 sprig thyme
- 2 sprigs rosemary
- 3 carrots, peeled and finely sliced into rounds
- sea salt and black pepper

1. Dust the sardines in the seasoned flour, and fry them in 2 tbsp of the olive oil for 2 minutes on both sides. (You do not need to cook the sardines all the way through at this point.) Lay the sardines in a dish 5cm deep.
2. Heat the rest of the ingredients in a small pan and simmer for 15 minutes. While still hot, pour over the fish. This will finish cooking the sardines. Season with salt and pepper.
3. Leave to marinate in the fridge, preferably overnight.
4. The olive oil mixture will have set in the fridge, so make sure you take the dish out of the fridge at least 1 hour before serving, to bring the dish back up to room temperature.

DAVINA MULFORD

Marinated chicken
with a yoghurt sauce and two salsas

Serves 6   Preparation time: 15 minutes, + 2 hours marinating
Cooking time: 10 minutes

- 6 skinless chicken breasts
- 6 tbsp olive oil
- Handful fresh thyme leaves
- zest and juice of 3 limes + several more limes to serve
- 2 mangoes
- 1 tbsp chopped mint
- 200g Greek yoghurt
- 3 tbsp chives, chopped
- 4 very ripe tomatoes
- 1 small red onion, finely chopped
- ½ bunch of basil, chopped
- pinch of sugar
- 1 tbsp mild olive oil
- sea salt and black pepper

1. Put the chicken between 2 pieces of baking or greaseproof paper and bash with a rolling pin until flat. In a bowl mix the olive oil, thyme, half the lime zest and juice, and a good grind of salt and pepper. Leave the flattened chicken pieces in the marinade for 2 hours.
2. To make the mango salsa, finely chop the mango flesh into a bowl. Add the chopped mint, and the remaining lime zest and juice. Set aside.
3. For the yoghurt sauce, mix together the yoghurt, chopped chives and season with salt and pepper.
4. Finally, for the tomato salsa, finely chop the tomatoes and add the chopped red onion, basil, a pinch of sugar, and salt and pepper to taste.
5. Add a tablespoon of oil to a frying pan and cook the chicken for 2 minutes on both sides at a high heat, before turning the heat down to cook the chicken through for a further 3 to 4 minutes, or until cooked through.
6. Serve with wedges of lime, new potatoes, couscous, bulgar wheat or fresh bread.

SARAH WILLES

Zinnia's linguine
with parsley, garlic, lemon and capers

One night in Italy, my friend Nick Gibbins cooked this delicious pasta as a starter to fish and it has remained a store cupboard winner ever since. It has a depth that belies the simple ingredients: the chilli and garlic give it a rich heat kick, while the two green elements, capers and parsley, bring freshness and zing. A little lemon juice, loads of parmesan and extra olive oil finish it off and will have you running your finger around the plate when you've finished.

Serves 4–6 as a starter   Preparation time: 15 minutes   Cooking time: 12 minutes

- 400g linguine
- 6 tablespoons olive oil
- 3 cloves garlic, crushed
- 2 medium red chillis, finely diced, or ½ tsp dried chilli flakes
- 1 bunch parsley
- 70g capers
- 1 lemon, juiced
- parmesan
- sea salt and black pepper

1. Cook the linguine in a large pan of salted boiling water. (Refer to packet for exact cooking times.)
2. While the pasta is cooking, heat the olive oil very gently in a large saucepan. Add the crushed garlic and chilli. Be careful not to let the garlic brown or it will taste bitter.
3. Roughly chop the parsley and capers.
4. Once the linguine has cooked, drain and add it to the olive oil mixture, along with the capers, parsley, salt, pepper and a good squeeze of lemon, to taste.
5. Serve immediately with some grated parmesan.

Helpful Hints:
❖ For a main course, you could add cooked prawns or clams to this dish.

ZINNIA SWANZY

Zinnia's linguine with parsley, garlic, lemon and capers, p.50

51

Turmeric chicken

Summer, summer, summer. Perfect with a watercress salad and new potatoes.

Serves 6   Preparation time: 10 minutes   Cooking time: 25–30 minutes

- 6 tbsp natural yoghurt
- 1 tsp turmeric
- juice of 2 lemons
- 1 tsp ground cardamom
- 2 cloves of garlic, finely chopped
- 2 tbsp olive oil
- 6 large chicken breasts, skin on
- chopped flat-leaf parsley or coriander

1. Preheat the oven to 180°/gas mark 4.
2. In a large bowl, mix together the yoghurt, turmeric, lime juice, cardamom, garlic and one tablespoon of olive oil.
3. Lay the chicken breasts in an ovenproof dish, skin sides up. Cover them with the yoghurt mixture and leave to marinade as long as you can, although this is not essential.
4. When you are ready, cook the chicken in the oven for 25–30 minutes, or until cooked through.
5. Serve the chicken in the dish with a large watercress salad, and scatter over the chopped parsley or coriander.

BLUES

Baked lemon fish with tomato sauce

A vibrant, healthy, summer dish. Serve with the quinoa tabbouleh on page 46, or fresh bread to soak up the sauce.

Serves 4–6 people   Preparation time: 20 minutes   Cooking time: 15–20 minutes

- 4 tbsp olive oil, plus extra to drizzle
- 2 red onions, diced
- 1 red chilli, deseeded and finely sliced
- 4 cloves garlic, crushed
- 10 fresh tomatoes, peeled and diced
- 1 tbsp tomato puree
- 100g Kalamata olives (pitted)
- juice of 1–2 lemons
- 4–6 pieces of cod, haddock or any other firm white fish
- 1 bunch basil, roughly chopped
- 1 small bunch parsley, roughly chopped
- sea salt and black pepper

1. Preheat the oven to 180°C/gas mark 4.
2. Heat the oil in a heavy-based pan. Add the chopped onion, chilli and garlic, and cook until they start to soften.
3. Add the chopped tomatoes, tomato purée and olives, and simmer the sauce for around 10 minutes until it starts to thicken slightly and come together.
4. Add the juice of half a lemon, and season with salt and pepper.
5. Spoon a layer of tomato sauce into the bottom of an ovenproof dish. Lay the fish over the tomato sauce. Squeeze the rest of the lemon juice over the fish and season it well with salt and pepper. Add the remaining tomato sauce over the top, drizzle it with a little olive oil and bake in the oven for 15–20 minutes, until the fish is just starting to flake when you touch it.
6. Top the dish with plenty of chopped basil and parsley, and serve.

Healthy Hints:

❖ Don't hold back from using any seafood or fish you like – this recipe is very flexible.

KALI HAMM

Alaphia's mujadara pilaf

This is a variation of the Lebanese dish mujadara, which I made up to accompany barbecued lamb cutlets.

Serves 6   Preparation time: 30 minutes   Cooking time: 1 hour

- 200g green cracked wheat (freekeh) or bulgar wheat
- 200g pearl barley
- 200g brown lentils
- 3 green cardamom pods
- 1 tsp coriander seeds
- 1 tsp cumin seeds
- 2 cinnamon sticks
- 150 ml olive oil + 3 tbsp olive oil
- 2 large onions
- 4 cloves garlic
- 2 large handfuls of golden sultanas
- zest of 1 orange
- 250ml chicken, vegetable or lamb stock
- sea salt to taste

1. Put the lentils, cracked wheat and pearl barley in to a large saucepan, and cover them with plenty of cold water, rinsing and refilling if the water seems cloudy.
2. Add a teaspoon of salt, the cardamom, coriander and cumin seeds, and the cinnamon sticks. Bring the pan to the boil, and leave it to simmer until the pulses are 'al dente', which should take about 25–30 minutes.
3. Drain and pour over the olive oil, stir and set aside.
4. Peel the onions and garlic. Cut the onions in half and slice them into semicircles, and slice the garlic lengthways. Fry them in 3 tablespoons of olive oil until golden. Add the sultanas, orange zest and stock to the fried onions, and leave to simmer for approximately 10 minutes, until the sauce has reduced.
5. Pour the mixture over the lentils, check the seasoning and add salt if you need to. Serve either hot or at room temperature.

Helpful Hints:

- ❖ This is very versatile, and ingredients can be added or replaced. Butternut squash, cut into small cubes, is a good addition, along with pieces of lamb.
- ❖ This recipe can be easily halved, doubled or quadrupled.
- ❖ Serve this with grilled meats and baked fish. Another good accompaniment is a salad made up of radishes, cucumber, chopped dill, chopped mint and a pungent lemon juice vinaigrette.

ALAPHIA BIDWELL

Courgette and orzo bake

This is a really easy dish to make and a great accompaniment to any barbecued fish or meat. Perfect for a children's supper too (perhaps omitting the wine!).

Serves 4–6   Preparation time: 20 minutes   Cooking time: 25 minutes

- 2–3 tbsp olive oil
- 2 onions, chopped finely
- 3 garlic cloves, crushed
- 500g courgettes, grated
- 500g orzo, krithraki or small macaroni
- 1 litre of vegetable or chicken stock
- small glass of white wine
- ½ tsp oregano, chopped finely
- 175g parmesan, grated
- 100g white breadcrumbs
- A good drizzle of extra virgin olive oil

1. Preheat the oven to 180°C/gas mark 4.
2. Butter a large 25–30cm ovenproof serving dish.
3. Heat the olive oil in a large pan and soften the onions, garlic and grated courgettes for about 10 minutes.
4. Stir in the orzo, stock, wine and oregano, and continue to cook for a couple of minutes.
5. Take off the heat, stir in half the parmesan, season and transfer to the serving dish. Scatter over the breadcrumbs and remaining parmesan, drizzle with the extra virgin olive oil. Bake for 25 minutes, or until the orzo is cooked. If the top has not browned by the time the orzo has cooked, pop under the grill for a couple of minutes until golden.

VICKY POWER

Chilli and Tarragon Chicken, p.57

Chilli and tarragon chicken

Serves 4   Preparation time: 10 minutes   Cooking time: 30–40 minutes

- zest of 1 lemon
- 1½ fresh red chillis, de-seeded and chopped
- 2 cloves of garlic, crushed or grated
- 4 tbsp olive oil
- 1 bunch fresh tarragon, approximately 20g
- 1 whole chicken, or 4–6 breasts or thighs
- 300ml natural yoghurt
- sea salt and freshly ground black pepper

1. Preheat the oven to 200°C/gas mark 6.
2. Mix together in a bowl the lemon zest, chopped chilli, garlic, olive oil and half the chopped tarragon. Season with sea salt and black pepper.
3. If you are using a whole chicken, joint the chicken and lay the pieces in a roasting tin, or lay out the breast or thigh pieces. Rub the chicken all over with the mixture.
4. Put the chicken in the oven to cook for 30–40 minutes, or until the skin is golden and it is cooked through.
5. Meanwhile mix the yoghurt with the remaining tarragon, and serve alongside the chicken.

Helpful Hints:
❖ Serve the chicken with the Greek beans on page 58.
❖ Add more or less of the tarragon and chilli, according to taste.
❖ Substitute tarragon with thyme, if you wish.

EMMA SCHUSTER

Greek beans

These beans make a lovely summery accompaniment to barbecued fish or chicken.

Serves 4   Preparation time: 5 minutes   Cooking time: 15 minutes

- 2 medium onions
- 2 tbsp olive oil
- 3 large ripe tomatoes
- 150ml water
- 300g whole trimmed green beans
- pinch of sugar
- 1 clove garlic, crushed
- sea salt and black pepper

1. Peel and halve the onions, and then slice thinly into semicircles. Heat the olive oil in a pan, add the onions and cook until they start to soften.
2. Roughly chop the tomatoes – no need to peel – and add them to the pan, along with the water and the beans. Season with salt and pepper, add a pinch of sugar and the garlic.
3. Bring up to the boil and simmer gently for 10–15 minutes, stirring from time to time. You may find that you need to add more water during this time – top up as necessary.

EMMA SCHUSTER

Sonia's poached peaches, p.60 and Soplillos granadinos, p.61

Sonia's poached peaches

Serves 4   Preparation time: 5 minutes   Cooking time: 10 minutes

- 4 to 6 whole peaches, skins on
- 1 vanilla pod
- 250ml water
- 120g caster sugar

1. Mix together the water and sugar in a medium-sized saucepan. Run a knife down the length of the vanilla pod, and scrape out the vanilla seeds from the inside. Add the seeds to the pan, along with the pod itself, and bring the contents to a gentle boil.
2. Place the whole peaches in the pan, and allow to cook in the sugar syrup for approximately 10 minutes, or until the peaches are soft and the skins are starting to wrinkle.
3. Remove the peaches and set them aside on a plate. Reduce liquid down to approximately 100ml. Return the peaches to the syrup and let them cool.

Helpful Hints:
- ❖ Add passion fruit to the syrup, once it has reduced, if you want to add a bit more to the pudding.
- ❖ Serve the peaches with mascarpone and soplillos granadinos (see p. 61).

SONIA TYSHING

Soplillos granadinos

These almond meringues are particularly good served with sultanas soaked in Pedro Jimenez sherry, or with Sonia's peaches (see p. 60).

Makes 10 large or 20 small meringues   Preparation time: 20 minutes
Cooking time: 30–40 minutes

- 200g whole blanched almonds
- 3 egg whites
- pinch of salt
- 250g caster sugar
- zest of 1 lemon

1. Preheat the oven to 150°C/gas mark 2.
2. Line 2 baking trays with baking paper.
3. Cook the almonds in a hot oven for about 10 minutes, or until lightly toasted.
4. Once they have cooled down, whiz the toasted almonds in a food processor until they are the size of pine nuts.
5. In a large clean, dry bowl, whisk the egg whites until stiff. Add the salt and half the sugar, and whisk until very stiff and shiny. Add the lemon zest, remaining sugar and almonds, and fold in using a large metal spoon.
6. Using 2 dessert spoons, shape the mixture into 10 or 20 meringues, and bake in the oven for 30–40 minutes. Once cooked, the meringues should lift easily off the baking paper, but still be soft in the middle.

JANE O'BRIEN

Orange and almond cake

Serve this as a pudding when it is still warm. A bowl of slightly sweetened crème fraîche and another of segmented oranges, and you are in heaven.
Use blood oranges if you possibly can.

Serves 6–8   Preparation time: 10 minutes   Cooking time: 30–40 minutes

- 100g softened butter
- 175g caster sugar
- 3 eggs, whisked together with a fork
- zest and juice of 2 oranges
- 100g ground almonds
- 1 tsp baking powder
- 50g plain flour
- 50g icing sugar

1. Preheat the oven to 180°C/gas mark 4.
2. Line and grease a loose 50 cm bottomed tin.
3. Cream together the butter and sugar together until light and fluffy. Slowly add the whisked eggs, and then gradually add half the orange zest and juice you have prepared. Mix well to prevent the mixture splitting.
4. Gently fold in the almonds, baking powder and flour, and combine well.
5. Pour into the prepared tin and bake for around 30–40 minutes until golden.
6. To make the drizzle, mix together the remaining orange zest and juice with the icing sugar in a small pan, and warm through, making sure the sugar has fully dissolved.
7. When the cake is cooked, remove it from the oven and allow to cool on a wire rack in the tin. Make little holes on the top of the cake with a skewer and pour over the drizzle while the cake is still warm.

ALISON RAVENSCROFT

Chocolate, coffee and pecan tart

Extremely rich and smooth. Perfect eaten very cold on a hot Mediterranean night with a cup of black coffee, when you need a bit of a pick-me-up to keep the party going.

Serves 6–8 people   Preparation time: 15 minutes + 15 blind baking time
Cooking time: 25–30 minutes

- 200g amaretti or digestive biscuits, crushed
- 100g butter
- 140g dark chocolate
- 115g butter
- 100g caster sugar
- 150ml maple syrup
- 2 tbsp of brandy
- 2½ tsp espresso coffee
- ¾ tsp of ground cinnamon
- 4 eggs
- 100g pecan nuts

1. Preheat the oven to 170°C/gas mark 3.
2. Blitz the biscuits in a food processor until in crumbs, or break them up in a plastic bag with a rolling pin. Melt 100g of butter and mix well with the biscuit crumbs.
3. Press the biscuit base into the base of an 20cm non-stick tart case, and place in the fridge to cool.
4. Melt the chocolate and butter in a bowl placed over a pan of simmering water, until smooth. In another saucepan heat the sugar and maple syrup until gently bubbling. Make sure that the sugar has completely melted, and then add it to the chocolate and butter mixture.
5. In a large bowl whisk together the brandy, espresso, cinnamon and eggs. Add the chocolate mixture and whisk until well combined. Lightly toast the pecan nuts in a dry frying pan, and place them on the biscuit base in the tart tin.
6. Carefully pour the mixture over the top, and bake for 25–30 minutes until just set. Allow it to cool completely before serving, and place in the fridge, if you have time. It will keep for a few days.

EMMA TINNE

White chocolate and amaretti torte

A more luxurious dinner time brother to the cheesecake. Indulge yourself, and keep it away from the children.

Serves 8–10   Preparation time: 10 minutes

- 100g butter and a little extra for the tin
- 200g Amaretti biscuits + 3 extra
- 350g white chocolate
- 550ml whipping cream (if in France and the cream won't whip, use mascarpone and pouring cream)

1. Grease a 25cm loose-bottomed tin.
2. In a food processor, whizz the biscuits so that they resemble breadcrumbs.
3. Melt the butter and mix with the biscuit crumbs. Press this mixture in to the tin and chill.
4. Melt the chocolate with a little runny cream in a bowl suspended over a pan of barely simmering water. Don't be alarmed if the melted chocolate is slightly lumpy. Leave to cool very slightly and whip the rest of the cream to form soft peaks.
5. Mix the chocolate mixture into the cream and spoon onto the biscuit base. Roughly crush the 3 extra Amaretti biscuits and sprinkle over the top. Cover and leave to cool in the fridge.
6. Serve with berries or peaches.

Helpful Hints:
❖ If you can't get hold of Amaretti biscuits, ginger biscuits work just as well, but you will lose the bold almond flavour that works so well.

POLLY PARSONS

Goulash soup, p.68

65

The Mountains and Countryside

We tend to associate cooking and eating on a mountain or country holiday with autumn or winter, and warming and plentiful dishes – food that will fill you up, has taken hours of slow cooking to come to fruition, and is comforting yet sustaining. These are holidays where we can cook and eat at leisure, before heading out for a day of walking, hiking, skiing, exploring or, best of all, sitting in front of a fire with a good book.

This chapter will arm you with an array of recipes for soups, stews, easy to prepare slow-cooks and one-dish meals, using ingredients that are generally available whether you are in the Swiss Alps or the Peak District.

Baked vacherin

This is great to have with pre-dinner drinks, and can be served with bread, cooked new potatoes, or crudités to dip into it.

Serves 4–6   Preparation time: 5 minutes   Cooking time: 15 minutes

- 1 x 500g vacherin cheese
- 2 tbsp dry white wine
- A few sprigs of rosemary or thyme

1. Preheat the oven to 180°C/gas mark 4.
2. Wrap the bottom of the cheese box in foil and sit the box inside the lid.
3. Cut slashes in the top of the cheese and add the wine. Stick the rosemary or thyme sprigs into the cheese.
4. Place the cheese on a baking tray and cook in the oven for 15 minutes, until melted and bubbling.

Helpful Hints:

❖ If you can't get vacherin, a camembert would also work well.

DAVINA MULFORD

Goulash soup

This hearty soup is a meal in itself, and is perfect for cold winter days.

Serves 4–6   Preparation time: 25 minutes   Cooking time: 2–2½ hours

- 3 tbsp olive oil
- 250g onions, sliced into semicircles
- 1 red pepper, deseeded and diced
- 3 large garlic cloves, crushed
- 500g stewing beef, cut into small cubes
- 1 heaped tbsp smoked paprika
- 1.2 litres of beef stock
- 1½ tbsp chopped oregano or marjoram
- 1½ caraway seeds
- 1 tbsp red wine vinegar
- 2 large tomatoes, peeled and chopped into dice
- 1 tbsp tomato puree
- 250g potatoes, peeled and diced
- sour cream (optional)
- chopped parsley (optional)
- sea salt and black pepper

1. Heat the olive oil in a large heavy-bottomed pan, and add the sliced onions, pepper and crushed garlic. Cook them gently, until they start to soften. Add the cubed beef, stir well and allow the meat to brown.
2. Stir in the smoked paprika and cook for a few minutes. Add half the beef stock, bring it to the boil and let it bubble for 10–15 minutes, until it is reduced by approximately half.
3. Add the oregano or marjoram, caraway seeds, red wine vinegar, chopped tomatoes and tomato puree, and season well with salt and pepper.
4. Cover the soup with more of the stock – enough to cover the meat and vegetables generously. Stir well and simmer for 1½ to 2 hours, or until the beef is tender.
5. Add the cubed potatoes, and allow them to cook for 20–30 minutes, or until soft. The soup will thicken considerably at this stage, so add any remaining stock if you need to.
6. Check the seasoning, and serve with crusty bread, a spoonful of sour cream, and a sprinkle of fresh parsley.

Helpful Hints:

❖ As with most stews and soups, this is best made a day or more in advance of when you want to eat it.
❖ Use tinned tomatoes if you do not have fresh ones.

HATTIE DEARDS

Pea and ham soup

This recipe has been kindly donated by the team at Brindisa – the home of Spanish food in London, sourcing foods from 80 of Spain's finest producers.

Served with a hunk of raw ewe's milk cheese such as roncal or villarejo manchego, and a slice of griddled sourdough drizzled with olive oil, this soup can be dressed up to make a rustic, informal supper.

Serves 4-6   Preparation time: 10 minutes   Cooking time: 20 minutes

- 2 tbsp olive oil
- 500g smoked pancetta
- 1 large onion, diced
- 900g frozen peas
- 1 litre ham stock or water
- small handful of roughly chopped mint
- sea salt and black pepper

1. Heat the olive oil in a large non-stick saucepan. Fry the diced pancetta until nicely browned and just turning crispy. Remove from the pan and set aside.
2. Use the oil and meat juices left in the pan (adding more oil if necessary) to sweat the onion.
3. Add the frozen peas and stock or water, bring to the boil, and simmer until the frozen peas are tender (about 10 mins).
4. Remove the pan from the heat. Add the mint and allow to cool slightly. Season to taste.
5. Puree in a blender, and serve with the cooked pancetta sprinkled on top.

BRINDISA

Diana's easy bread recipe

Preparation time: 15 minutes, plus 30 minutes proving
Makes: 1 medium-sized loaf   Cooking time: 45 minutes

- 1tbsp brown sugar
- 400ml warm water
- 400g malt flour
- 300g strong white bread flour
- 1tbsp salt
- 1tsp dried yeast

1. Preheat the oven to 50°C/gas mark ¼.
2. Add the sugar to the water to dissolve, giving it a quick stir.
3. Mix together all the other ingredients in a bowl, stirring in the sweetened water to bring the mixture together. Add more water if necessary.
4. Kneed the dough for 15 minutes on a lightly floured surface. Shape the dough into a round loaf and place on a baking tray. Sprinkle with a little flour: you can also cut slashes into the top if you are feeling creative. Put it on a baking tray and into a warm oven of 50°C to prove for 30 minutes.
5. After 30 minutes, increase the temperature to 200°C/gas mark 6 and cook for a further 45 minutes. To test if the bread is cooked, tap the bottom of the loaf – it should sound hollow.

Helpful Hints:

❖ You can also sprinkle poppy or sesame seeds on top, if you like.

DIANA HORSFORD

Beetroot and roquefort salad

This salad goes particularly well with rare roast beef. Alternatively, serve as a starter with some warm bread and butter.

Serves 4–6 Preparation time: 10 minutes

- 8 medium-sized cooked beetroots
- 4 tbsp red wine vinegar
- 4 tbsp walnut oil
- 100g toasted, chopped walnuts
- 125g roquefort cheese
- a handful of flat-leaf parsley, roughly chopped
- freshly ground black pepper

1. Peel the beetroots, if you need to, and cut into matchstick-sized pieces. In a bowl mix the beetroot with the vinegar, oil and pepper.
2. Toss the walnuts and the parsley with the beetroot and arrange in a shallow serving dish. Crumble the roquefort evenly over the top and serve.

SARAH WILLES

Goat's cheese and thyme soufflé

Sally Clarke used to be a Blues cook, before setting up Clarke's restaurant and shop in Kensington in 1984.

Many people are nervous about making soufflés at home, but this one is simple and tastes heavenly.

Serves 4–6   Preparation time: 15 minutes   Cooking time: 8-10 minutes

- 30g butter
- 200g grated parmesan
- 6 eggs
- 400g soft goat's cheese
- 150ml double cream
- 1 tsp chopped thyme
- a few thyme leaves
- sea salt and back pepper

1. Preheat the oven to 200°C/gas mark 6.
2. Butter 6 ovenproof soup plates or ramekins. Sprinkle with a quarter of the parmesan. Separate the eggs into 2 bowls.
3. Whisk the egg yolks until smooth, add the goat's cheese and whisk again. Stir in the cream and season with the chopped thyme and salt and pepper. Fold in half the remaining parmesan.
4. In a separate clean, dry bowl, whisk the egg whites until stiff peaks are formed. Fold the whites thoroughly into the cheese mixture, divide between the dishes and sprinkle with any remaining thyme leaves and parmesan.
5. Place on a baking sheet in the oven and bake for approximately 8–10 minutes until risen and golden. Serve immediately, reminding guests that the dishes are oven hot!

Helpful Hints:

❖ You could also serve this in a large 25cm x 30cm ovenproof dish.
❖ This recipe works well with feta cheese instead of goat's cheese, but it does give a stronger flavour and needs less salt.

SALLY CLARKE

George's reblochon potatoes

This is a cheat's version of tartiflette – highly calorific, and the ultimate comfort food.

Reblochon is an Alpine cheese from the Haute-Savoie region of France. It is a creamy washed-rind cow's milk cheese. You can find it in most of the larger supermarkets in the UK.

Serves 4–6 Preparation time: 20 minutes Cooking time: 2–3 minutes

- 1kg new potatoes
- 200g smoked lardons
- 1 small bunch of spring onions
- 250ml crème fraiche
- 1 tsp wholegrain mustard
- 250g reblochon cheese, sliced
- a squeeze of lemon
- sea salt and black pepper

1. Boil the new potatoes until just cooked.
2. Fry the lardons in a dry pan until golden.
3. Cut the potatoes in half and mix them in a bowl with spring onions, crème fraiche and mustard.
4. Pour the potato mixture into a shallow ovenproof dish, and top with the slices of reblochon.
5. Place under a hot grill and cook for 2–3 minutes, or until the cheese is golden and bubbling. Serve immediately.

GEORGINA BERKLEY

George's reblochon potatoes, p.73
Sweet potato and pancetta gratin, p.75

Sweet potato and pancetta gratin

Deliciously comforting and indulgent, this is a perfect accompaniment to roast chicken.

Serves 4–6   Preparation time: 25 minutes   Cooking time: 1 hour, approx

- 4 medium sweet potatoes, approximately 1kg
- 140g cubed pancetta or smoked bacon cut into cubes
- 1 large handful of chopped sage, approximately 20g
- 4 cloves of garlic, crushed
- 500ml single cream
- sea salt and black pepper

1. Preheat the oven to 200°C/gas mark 6.
2. Wash the sweet potatoes and remove any fibres or eyes, but do not peel them. Cut them into thin disks, ½cm thick, with a sharp knife, or use a mandolin if you have one.
3. Cook the pancetta or bacon in a dry frying pan, until crisp. Chop the sage roughly, and crush or grate the garlic.
4. Arrange the slices of sweet potato in a deep, medium-sized oven dish. Stack the slices in rows, skin side showing, and intermittently scatter the cooked pancetta and chopped sage. Season well with sea salt and freshly ground black pepper.
5. Cover the dish with tin foil and cook in the oven for 40 minutes.
6. Mix together the cream with the crushed garlic, and season lightly with salt and pepper. Pour the cream over the potatoes after 40 minutes of cooking time, and return to the oven – uncovered – for another 30 minutes.

Helpful Hints:
❖ You can substitute the sweet potato with butternut squash. If you go for this option you might want to omit the sage and add a handful of grated parmesan instead.

HATTIE DEARDS

Jo's courgette carbonara

This is a firm hit every time with adults and children. If you buy your courgettes from a local market and they still have their flowers intact, include them in the recipe as they will look beautiful.

Serves 4   Preparation time: 10 minutes   Cooking time: 20 minutes

- 1 tsp olive oil
- 10 rashers of smoked streaky bacon
- 4 medium green and yellow (if available) courgettes, cut into batons
- a sprig of fresh or 1 tsp of dried thyme
- 400g penne
- 4 free-range egg yolks
- 100ml of double cream
- 100g of freshly grated parmesan
- sea salt and black pepper

1. Put a large pan of water on the hob to boil, and add a teaspoon of salt.
2. Cut the bacon into squares, and fry in the olive oil in a non-stick frying pan. Once the bacon has begun to cook, add the courgette batons, a good twist of black pepper and the fresh or dried thyme. Regularly turn the courgette and bacon mixture so that every-thing takes on golden colour.
3. Add the penne to the boiling water, stir well and cook according to packet instructions. Do not overcook it – it should be al dente. While the pasta is cooking, mix together the cream, egg yolks and parmesan cheese in a separate bowl.
4. Drain the pasta when just cooked, keeping back approximately 200ml of the cooking water.
5. Turn the heat off the frying pan, and add the pasta to the bacon and courgettes. Add the carbonara sauce and a little of the pasta water, stirring to coat all the penne. Add a little more pasta water to create a silky smooth sauce. (Do not put the pasta back on the heat as it will scramble the eggs.)
6. Serve immediately on warmed plates with extra freshly grated parmesan if desired, and season to taste with salt and black pepper.

JO PRESTON

Slow-cooked beef ragu

Because this is a slow-cook recipe and needs very little attention, you can either show off and make homemade pasta to serve with it, or you can go out and spend the day with your family or friends, knowing you have something delicious to come home to.

Serves 4–6 Preparation time: 20 minutes Cooking time: 4–5 hours

- 1 tbsp olive oil
- 20 baby onions or shallots peeled and left whole
- 150g pancetta, cubed
- 3 cloves of garlic, thinly sliced
- 1kg of chuck beef steak, cut into big 8cm cubes
- 500ml good red wine
- 300ml beef or chicken stock
- 300g ripe cherry tomatoes
- 3 bay leaves
- sprig of thyme
- 3 juniper berries – optional
- 1 tsp ground cinnamon, or one cinnamon stick
- 1 heaped tbsp redcurrant jelly
- 1 tsp English mustard
- parsley stalks – if you have them
- 20g butter
- sea salt and black pepper

1. Preheat the oven to 150°C/gas mark 2.
2. Heat a tablespoon of olive oil in a large frying pan. Add the shallots and pancetta, and cook until they start to colour. Add the garlic and cook for a further 2 minutes, and then transfer to a casserole dish.
3. Brown the meat in the same pan, and add the wine. Heat until bubbling and then add the meat and wine to the casserole dish.
4. Add the remaining ingredients, apart from the butter, stir well and season with salt and pepper. Bring to a gentle boil on the hob, then cover with a lid or double-layered aluminium foil, and place in the oven.
5. Cook the ragu slowly for 4–5 hours (reduce the heat if it is bubbling ferociously in the oven), and check it every now and then to ensure there is just enough liquid to cover the beef, and top it up with wine or stock as necessary.
6. Once the beef is tender enough to shred, remove it from the liquid. Add the butter to the cooking liquor and reduce it by a third.
7. Shred the beef with a couple of forks and add it to the reduced sauce, removing any bay leaves or stalks, and stir thoroughly. Season with salt and pepper if necessary.
8. Keep the ragu in the fridge until ready to reheat. Serve with pappardelle, tagliatelle or other wide ribbon pasta, and add lots of parmesan.

Helpful Hints:

❖ If you do not have any red wine to hand, use white instead. The flavour will be slightly different, but just as delicious.

ELIZABETH CURTIS

Whole trout with tomatoes and herbs

This recipe has been kindly donated by Fiona Burrell from Edinburgh New Town Cookery School.

Serves 4   Preparation time: 10 minutes   Cooking time: 15 minutes, approx

- 4 small trout, rainbow or brown, cleaned
- finely grated zest of 1 lemon
- 2 tbsp lemon juice
- 1 large clove garlic, crushed
- 3 tbsp finely chopped mixed herbs, e.g. parsley, chives, mint, tarragon
- 5 tbsp rapeseed or olive oil
- 12 cherry tomatoes, halved
- sea salt and black pepper

1. Preheat the oven to 200°C/gas mark 6.
2. With a sharp knife make 3 diagonal slashes through the skin down each side of the trout.
3. In a bowl, mix the lemon zest, juice, garlic, herbs and oil together. Season with salt and pepper. It should taste quite lemony without being too sharp, so add a little more olive oil if necessary.
4. Lay out 4 large pieces of aluminium foil on the worktop. Rub the herb mixture inside the cavity and on the sides of the fish. Place each fish on the aluminium foil and put 6 cherry tomatoes halves in each cavity.
5. Wrap up and seal well.
6. Place the parcels on a baking tray and cook in the oven for 15 minutes, or until cooked.
7. Open the parcels and serve. Serve with homemade mayonnaise or hollandaise sauce.

Helpful Hints:

- ❖ The trout parcels can be prepared up to 30 minutes before cooking to let the flavours infuse.
- ❖ They can also be cooked on a barbecue in the summer – just turn the parcels over halfway through cooking.

FIONA BURRELL

Chestnut bourguignon

A vegetarian version of the classic Boeuf bourguignon. Serve it with a mountain of mashed potatoes.

Serves 4–6   Preparation time: 20 minutes   Cooking time: 1–1½ hours

- 2 tbsp olive oil
- 300g button onions, peeled
- 200g carrots
- 2 cloves garlic, crushed
- 500ml red wine
- 1 x 400g tin tomatoes
- 300g peeled chestnuts
- 200g brown mushrooms or field mushrooms, quartered
- 1 bay leaf
- 2 sprigs thyme (or a large pinch of dried thyme)
- 1 level dsp tomato ketchup
- 250ml–500ml vegetable stock
- pinch of ground nutmeg
- ½ bunch parsley
- sea salt and black pepper

1. Heat the olive oil in a large saucepan or casserole dish. Add the olive oil and onions and fry gently for 5 minutes until browned. Add the carrots, garlic, wine and tomatoes, and simmer for 20 minutes.
2. Add the chestnuts, mushrooms, bay leaf, thyme, nutmeg and ketchup. Season with salt and pepper, and add enough vegetable stock to cover all the ingredients generously. Allow to simmer gently for a further 50 minutes with the lid off, and add any remaining stock if it looks dry.
3. Make sure that the sauce is reduced enough. If not, simmer for longer. Check the seasoning, adding more nutmeg if needed.
4. Garnish with chopped parsley and serve.

SARAH WILLES

Paysanne chicken with puy lentils

*Homely, comforting, nutritious and the easiest
meal imaginable.*

Serves 6   Preparation time: 10 minutes   Cooking time: 1½ hours

- 4 leeks
- 3 celery sticks
- 2 large carrots
- 200g pancetta or smoked bacon
- 1 tbsp olive oil
- sprig of fresh thyme
- 175g puy lentils, rinsed
- 1 medium to large chicken, approx 2kg
- 800ml of chicken stock, approx
- parsley, roughly chopped
- sea salt and black pepper

1. Roughly chop the leeks, celery and carrots, and cut the bacon or pancetta into dice.
2. Heat the olive oil in a large casserole dish on the hob, and brown the bacon for two or three minutes.
3. Add the chopped vegetables, thyme and puy lentils, and place the whole chicken on top. Pour over the stock, making sure that you have enough that it comes half way up the chicken. Season the dish well with salt and pepper.
4. Cover the casserole with a tight-fitting lid and simmer on the hob top for an hour and a half, or place in the oven at 200°C/gas mark 6 for the same amount of time. You can remove the lid towards the end of the cooking time to allow the chicken to brown.
5. When cooked, remove the chicken from the casserole and cut up roughly into large pieces. Sprinkle the chopped parsley over the lentils and vegetables, and serve with the chicken in individual bowls with plenty of the delicious chicken broth.
6. Serve with fresh bread and a green vegetable if required.

Helpful Hints:

❖ If you don't have a casserole dish, use a deep roasting tin and cover the chicken with a double layer of tin foil to act as a lid.

JANINE DEWEY

Beef with red wine and prunes

This is a super, hearty, winter-warming classic. It can be prepared in advance and re-heated – ideal after a long day in the snow or out in the country.

Serves 4–6   Preparation time: 20 minutes   Cooking time: 2½ hours

- 1½kg of cubed stewing beef or whole topside – trimmed of fat and sinew
- 1 tbsp olive oil
- 1 onion, diced
- 4 cloves of garlic, sliced
- 2 carrots, cut into chunks on the diagonal
- 2 celery sticks, diced
- ½ tsp allspice
- 2 bay leaves
- 1 tbsp of tomato puree
- 250ml red wine
- 500ml beef stock
- 250g pitted prunes
- sea salt and black pepper

1. Preheat the oven to 170°C/gas mark 3.
2. Season the beef with salt and pepper. Heat a tablespoon of olive oil in a heavy-bottomed frying pan, and brown the meat all over. Put the meat into a large casserole dish.
3. Brown the onion, garlic, carrot and celery in the frying pan. Once they are a good colour, add the allspice, bay leaves, tomato puree, red wine and stock. Bring the ingredients to the boil and pour the whole lot over the beef in the casserole dish. Add the prunes, and cover the casserole with a lid.
4. Cook in the oven for approximately 2½ hours, or until the meat is really tender – you should be able to eat it with a spoon. The sauce should be rich and thick; if it is not take the meat out and reduce the sauce on the stove.
5. Pull the meat apart into large-ish pieces and serve with a large spoonful of the sauce.
6. Serve the beef with parmesan-laden polenta with lots of seasoning or mashed potato, and a green salad.

JO PRESTON

Chicken with white wine, leeks and mustard

Fantastically quick and easy, and equally good with warm bread or mashed potatoes.

Serves 4 Preparation time: 15 minutes Cooking time: 1 hour

- 8 chicken thighs, or a whole jointed chicken, if you prefer
- 1 tbsp olive oil
- 300ml dry white wine
- 4 leeks, trimmed and cut into large 5cm chunks
- 3 large cloves of garlic, crushed
- 4 sprigs of thyme
- 4 bay leaves
- 200ml chicken stock
- 2 heaped tbsp Dijon mustard
- large handful of chopped parsley
- sea salt and black pepper

1. Preheat the oven to 200°C/gas mark 6.
2. Season the chicken well on both sides with salt and pepper. Heat the olive oil in a large frying pan, and brown the chicken, skin side down, for 5 minutes or until golden brown. Transfer the chicken to an ovenproof dish or roasting tray. Tip away any fat in the pan.
3. Pour the wine into the frying pan, add the leeks, garlic, thyme, bay leaves and chicken stock. When it begins to bubble, pour the contents of the pan over the chicken, and arrange so that the leeks fall to the sides of the chicken. Cover with foil and cook in the oven for 30 minutes.
4. Remove the foil and cook for a further 30 minutes, making sure that the chicken skin is brown and crispy.
5. Pour the juices into a bowl and thoroughly whisk in the mustard and chopped parsley, and check the seasoning. Pour the juice back around the chicken and serve with warm crusty bread or a large bowl of mashed potatoes.

CATHY SYNAN

Slow-cooked pork with pumpkin

The largest pig I have ever seen was in Burma; she was over six feet long, about half as wide, and had seven tiny piglets, each one no bigger than their mother's nose. You see pigs wherever you go and pork is often cooked at home in stews and hotpots. This is a memory of a comforting, flavourful dish we enjoyed in 1981. The flavour is better still if you cook the dish the day before and reheat it. Rather than use tamarind pods, buy a jar of smooth tamarind purée, available in Asian shops and some supermarkets.

Serves 4   Preparation time: 15 minutes   Cooking time: 3 hours

- 2 onions
- 4 large cloves of garlic
- walnut-sized piece of fresh root ginger
- 750g boneless pork
- 3 tsp soft brown sugar
- 300g piece of skinned and deseeded pumpkin
- 2 tbsp groundnut oil
- 1 tsp chilli powder
- 1 tsp turmeric
- 300ml water
- 2 tbsp dark soy sauce
- 2 tbsp tamarind puree (if you can find it)
- 1 heaped tbsp of peanut butter
- large handful of coriander leaves

1. Peel, quarter and thinly slice the onions. Peel and chop the garlic finely, and peel the ginger and slice it into slivers. Cut the pork into 3cm pieces and sprinkle all over with the sugar.
2. Slice the pumpkin flesh into roughly equal-sized pieces.
3. Heat 1 tbsp of the groundnut oil in a fairly large casserole on a medium heat. Add the sugared pork and stir around quickly until browned all over, then remove the pork and set aside.
4. Heat the remaining tablespoon of oil in the casserole, add the onions and cook until soft and richly browned. Stir in the garlic, ginger, chilli powder and turmeric and cook, stirring, for another minute.
5. Remove from the heat, return the pork to the dish and add the pieces of pumpkin.
6. Heat the oven to 150°C/gas mark 2. Measure the water in a jug and stir in the soy sauce, tamarind purée (if you have it), and peanut butter. Pour into the casserole dish, stir and cover. Bring to a gentle bubble on the hob, and then place on a low shelf in the oven for 2½ hours, until the pork is very tender.
7. Check the seasoning and add more chilli and soy sauce if needed. Before serving, roughly chop the coriander leaves and stir them into the dish.

JOSCELINE DIMBLEBY Orchards in the Oasis, *Quadrille, 2010*

Pheasant with braised little gem lettuce, peas and bacon

A lovely way to serve pheasant, and pleasingly simple.

Serves 6   Preparation time: 15 minutes   Cooking time: 45 minutes

- 3 pheasants
- 1 tbsp olive oil
- 50g butter
- 1 onion or large shallot
- 2 large leeks
- 6–8 rashers of smoked streaky bacon
- 2 little gem lettuces
- 300g frozen peas
- sprig of fresh thyme, or 1 tsp of dried thyme
- 300ml double cream
- 100g grated parmesan
- sea salt and black pepper

1. Preheat the oven to 180°C/gas mark 4.
2. Season the pheasants with salt and pepper. Heat the olive oil in a large frying pan, and quickly brown the pheasants all over before putting them on a baking tray and cooking them in the oven for 30 minutes, until just cooked. Cover with tin foil and leave to rest for 15 minutes.
3. While the birds are in the oven, melt the butter in a large frying pan. Add the onion, leeks and bacon, and cook until they have coloured slightly and cooked down. Add the lettuce and the peas, along with the thyme, and stir well. Cook for a further 2 minutes, then add the cream and continue to stir until slightly thickened and bubbling.
4. Add the parmesan and any juices from the roasting pheasants, and season with salt and pepper to taste.
5. Remove the breasts from the pheasants, with the crispy skin still in place, and slice diagonally into thirds. Serve with the lettuce and pea cream, and sprinkle over any remaining thyme leaves.
6. Serve with new or mashed potatoes.

Helpful Hints:
❖ If you like the sound of this recipe but cannot get hold of pheasant, or don't like it, use chicken instead.

JOANNA PRESTON

Pork belly with fennel seeds and butter beans

This is one of my favourite recipes. It is easy to prepare, and needs very little attention during the cooking process – leaving you free to enjoy a bath or a glass of wine before dinner.

Serves 4–6   Preparation time: 10 minutes, plus 24 hours marinading time (optional)
Cooking time: 2½ hours

- 1½kg pork belly, bones removed and skin scored (keep the bones)
- 2 tbsp fennel seeds
- ½ tsp dried chilli flakes
- 1 tbsp chopped rosemary or thyme
- 3 cloves crushed garlic
- 3 tbsp olive oil
- 3 large onions
- 3 x 400g tins butter beans, drained
- 200g sun-blushed tomatoes
- ½ bunch flat-leaf parsley, roughly chopped
- sea salt and black pepper

1. In a small bowl, mix together the fennel seeds, chilli flakes, chopped rosemary, crushed garlic, olive oil, and a good grind of salt and pepper. Rub the mixture over the underside of the pork belly, and leave to marinate overnight.
2. Preheat the oven to 220°C/gas mark 7. Slice the onions and place them in the bottom of a roasting dish. Lay the pork bones, if you have them, on top of the onions, followed by the pork belly, skin-side up. Pat the skin dry of necessary.
3. Fill the roasting dish with water until it reaches the line of fat. Cook in the oven for 30 minutes, then turn the oven down to 150°C/gas mark 2 and cook for a further 2 hours.
4. Take the dish out of the oven. Lift out the pork belly out and set aside on a plate to keep warm, crisping up the crackling under the grill if necessary. Discard the bones from the baking dish, and pour the cooking liquid and onions into a saucepan.
5. Add the butter beans and sun-blushed tomatoes, and heat through on medium heat, making sure the butter beans are heated through. Add the roughly chopped parsley, and season further with salt and pepper if needed.
6. Slice the pork belly into 1cm thick slices and serve on warm plates, with a large spoonful of the butter beans and some purple-sprouting broccoli.

HELPFUL HINTS:

- ❖ If you are able to, ask your butcher to provide you with the bones from the pork belly as they add great flavour to the finished dish.
- ❖ If you are tight on fridge space, you don't have to marinate the pork overnight, but it will taste better if you do.

DAVINA MULFORD

Quick sticky toffee pudding

Unbelievably rich and indulgent, be prepared. Not for the faint-hearted.

Serves 6   Preparation time: 10 minutes   Cooking time: 15 minutes

- 2 McVities Jamaican ginger cakes
- 90g butter + extra for buttering the oven dish
- 300g brown sugar
- 300g golden syrup
- crème fraiche or natural yoghurt to serve
- 40g approximately of toasted and chopped pecans, or nuts of your choice, to sprinkle over the top

1. Pre heat the oven to 180°C/gas mark 4.
2. Cut the cakes into 2cm slices. Butter an ovenproof dish of any shape, but large enough so that you can lay the slices of cake in it with them slightly overlapping.
3. Put the butter, sugar and golden syrup into a small pan, and heat through until gently bubbling for about 5 minutes.
4. Pour the sauce over the cake, covering all the slices. Bake in the oven for 15 minutes.
5. Top with the crème fraiche and toasted nuts.

MICHELE HARRISON

Frangipani plum tart, p.89

Frangipani plum tart

*I made this in the Isle of Wight for a family who insisted I used
Mirabelle plums foraged from the local roundabout. But
should you come across some enticing-looking pears or
apricots, then use them instead.*

*This tart benefits from sitting in the pantry overnight so the
glaze seeps in. It is best eaten with crème anglaise, or
vanilla ice cream.*

Serves 10 people   Preparation time: 15 minutes   Cooking time: 50 minutes

- 1 roll of puff pastry
- 8 tbsp apricot or plum jam
- 200g softened butter
- 150g caster sugar
- 4 eggs
- 300g ground almonds
- seeds from 1 vanilla pod, or 1tbsp of vanilla extract
- zest of 1 lemon
- 10 plums stoned and halved, or 8 pears peeled and segmented, or 15 apricots/greengages halved
- 1 tbsp caster sugar
- 2 tbsp water
- A good splash of complementing liqueur, such as Poire Williams, Cointreau or Amaretto

1. Preheat the oven to 180°C/gas mark 4.
2. Roll the pastry very thin, and line a 26cm tart tin. Leave the 'overhang' in place for now. Prick the base well with a fork and spread the jam evenly. Return the lined tin to the fridge.
3. For the filling, beat together the butter and sugar using an electric beater or food processor. Slowly whisk in the eggs, and then the almonds, lemon zest and vanilla until creamy.
4. Take the tart case out of the fridge and trim off the excess pastry. Fill the tart case with the frangipane mixture. Arrange the fruit on top, so that the filling oozes between the fruit.
5. Bake for 50 minutes on the middle shelf of the oven until the filling is set and lightly golden.
6. While the tart is still hot, make the glaze by bringing the sugar and two tablespoons of water to the boil. Take the pan off the heat, add the alcohol and brush over the tart.

ELIZABETH CURTIS

Rhubarb crumble

An old classic. We have used rhubarb here, but you can use apples, blackberries, pears, plums, apricots, peaches – the options are endless.

Serves 4–6   Preparation time: 10 minutes   Cooking time: 45 minutes

- 700g rhubarb, trimmed
- 4 tbsp caster sugar
- 100g butter
- 150g plain flour
- large pinch cinnamon
- 50g chopped hazelnuts
- 50g oats
- 140g muscovado dark brown sugar

1. Preheat the oven to 180°C/gas mark 4.
2. Cut the rhubarb into 5cm pieces and place in the bottom of an ovenproof dish and sprinkle with caster sugar.
3. Put the butter and flour into a food processor and blitz until it is the consistency of large breadcrumbs. Tip the mixture into a large bowl, and stir in the cinnamon, nuts, oats, and muscovado sugar. This crumble mixture should be in clumps rather than fine bread crumbs; this will make it crunchy at the end.
4. Sprinkle the crumble mixture over the top of the rhubarb.
5. Lightly place a piece of foil over the top and cook in the oven for 30 minutes, then take the foil off and cook for a further 15 minutes.
6. Serve with crème fraiche, or praline ice-cream.

SARAH WILLES

Quick and easy cheesecake

*We had to include this cheesecake recipe in the book, as it is
such an old favourite. Since it requires no cooking, it
is easy to make with children.*

Serves 6–8   Preparation time: 15 minutes, + 1 hour chilling time

- 200g ginger biscuits
- 75g butter
- 400g cream cheese, preferably philadelphia
- 2 tbsp crème fraiche
- zest and juice of 1 lemon
- 75g caster sugar
- 2–3 tsp vanilla extract, or 1 tsp vanilla essence
- 150ml double or whipping cream
- 400g strawberries

1. Blitz the biscuits in a food processor until they resemble breadcrumbs and tip them into a bowl. Melt the butter and mix it thoroughly with the biscuit breadcrumbs. Press the biscuit mixture into the bottom of an 20cm loose-bottom cake tin. Put the base in the fridge to firm up.
2. In a large bowl, mix together the cream cheese, crème fraiche, lemon, sugar and vanilla. In a separate bowl whip the cream until it is thick, using an electric hand whisk.
3. Fold this into the cream cheese mixture, and pour the mixture into the cake tin. Place the tin in the fridge for as long as you can, so that it has time to firm up.
4. Hull and quarter the strawberries. Before serving the cheesecake, arrange the quarters in circles around the top of the cheesecake, with the points of the strawberries facing in.

Helpful Hints:

❖ If you don't have a food processor, you can break up the biscuits by putting them into a freezer bag and bashing them with a rolling pin. This produces slightly larger 'breadcrumbs' than using a food processor.
❖ If you are using vanilla essence, remember that this is a lot stronger than extract. Use to taste.

SARAH WILLES

Annabel's crostata with apples and mixed berries

A deliciously higgledy-piggledy tart, perfect for a winter's day. Feel free to substitute the apples and berries for another fruit of your choice.

Serves 6   Preparation time: 40 minutes   Cooking time: 30 minutes

- 200g plain flour
- 2 tbsp caster sugar
- pinch of sea salt
- 50g unsalted butter, chopped into pieces
- 7 tbsp freshly squeezed orange juice
- 200g blackberries
- 150g blueberries
- 150g raspberries
- 1 apple
- ½ tsp allspice

- ½ tsp nutmeg
- 1 tbsp cinnamon
- 5 tbsp caster sugar
- zest of ½ an orange
- zest of ½ a lemon
- 2 tbsp granulated sugar + extra for sprinkling
- 1 tbsp freshly squeezed orange juice
- 1 egg, beaten
- mascapone, to serve

1. Preheat the oven to 200°C/gas mark 6.
2. Put the flour, sugar and salt into the bowl of a food processor, and pulse in the butter, until the mixture resembles breadcrumbs. Gradually add the freshly squeezed orange juice and pulse again until the pastry comes together into a soft dough, adding more juice if you need to. This pastry can also be made by hand in a large mixing bowl.
3. Roll out the pastry onto a lightly floured piece of baking paper until you have a circle with a 30cm diameter (it does not have to be exact or a perfect circle). Transfer the pastry and baking paper onto a tray and chill in the fridge for 20 minutes.
4. While waiting for the pastry to cool, prepare your fruit. Peel and slice the apple, rinse the berries and set aside.
5. Mix together the allspice, nutmeg, cinnamon, sugar and lemon and orange zest in a bowl.
6. Keeping it on the baking paper, take your pastry from the fridge on its tray, and lightly mark a circle 5cm from the edge. This will later be used to enclose the fruit.
7. Within this circle sprinkle the base with the granulated sugar and spice mixture. On top of this, add the fruit mix followed by a tablespoon of orange juice.
8. Slowly fold up the edges of the pastry to create a case, which will keep all the fruit held in together. You should still be able to see most of the fruit from the top. Pinch the sides together to ensure a strong hold.
9. In a bowl lightly beat the egg, and lightly brush the edges of the pastry before it goes in the oven, adding a sprinkling of granulated sugar.
10. Cook in the oven for around 30 minutes, or until the fruit is cooked and the pastry is golden brown.
11. Serve with a dollop of mascarpone and a drizzle of honey.

ANNABEL GRAHAM-WOOD

Cakes
and bakes

Blueberry, bran and apple muffins

Healthy muffins are the ideal quick snack for children, and the lack of sugar will mean your holiday can continue harmoniously without any outbreaks of sugar-induced wildness.

Makes 12   Preparation time: 10 minutes Cooking time: 25–30 minutes

- 30g butter
- 250g honey
- 120ml milk
- 110ml vegetable oil
- 3 eggs
- 450g plain flour
- 2 tsp baking powder
- 100g bran
- 1½ tsp cinnamon
- 1 apple, grated
- 2 bananas, mashed
- 250g blueberries
- 4 figs

1. Preheat the oven to 180°C/gas mark 4. Line a muffin tray with paper muffin cases.
2. Melt the butter and honey in a saucepan.
3. In a bowl, whisk the milk, vegetable oil and eggs.
4. Place flour, baking powder, bran and cinnamon in a large bowl and mix. Stir in the apple, mashed banana and blueberries.
5. Make a well in the middle of the flour mixture and pour in the milk mixture. Using a wooden spoon, stir until just combined.
6. Fill the muffin cases with the mixture. Place a slice of fig on top of each one. Bake in the oven for 25–30 minutes.
7. To test if the muffins are cooked, insert a skewer – it should come out clean.

EMMA TINNE

Blackcurrant granola bars

This is a recipe that I created in an attempt to use up the surplus blackcurrants in my freezer. We had a glut from the garden: I ran out of ideas as how to use them, and this is the result.

Makes 8–12 bars   Preparation time: 5–10 minutes   Cooking time: 45 minutes

- 95g unsalted butter
- 95g soft brown sugar
- 95g maple syrup
- 45g chopped green pistachios
- 100g blackcurrants
- 45g pumpkin seeds
- 30g sesame seeds
- 30g ground almonds
- 190g rolled oats
- pinch of sea salt

1. Preheat the oven to 180°C/gas mark 4. Line a 20cm square oven tray with baking paper.
2. In a large pan melt the butter with the sugar and maple syrup until all the sugar has dissolved.
3. Add all the other ingredients and mix well.
4. Transfer the mixture to the lined baking tray and press into the tin. Bake for 45 minutes, or until golden brown on top, and cut into bars while still warm.

Helpful Hints:

- ❖ This benefits from being eaten on the day – ideally slightly warm.
- ❖ Play around with the mix of ingredients – add poppy seeds or use sour cherries, dried apricots and indeed fresh raspberries if you don't have any blackcurrants.

JOANNA PRESTON

Honey cake

This requires very few ingredients, and is nicely old fashioned. Delicious enjoyed at midday with a strong cup of coffee.

Serves 6–8   Preparation time: 15 minutes   Cooking time: 50–60 minutes

- 225g honey
- 225g butter
- 100g muscovado sugar
- 3 eggs
- 300g self-raising flour, sieved
- Grated zest of one lemon (optional)

1. Preheat oven to 140°C/gas mark 1. Grease a 20cm loose-bottomed cake tin with butter and line with baking paper.
2. Melt the honey, butter and sugar in a small pan. Allow to cool for 10 minutes, then beat in the eggs and fold in the sieved flour. Add the grated lemon rind at this point if using.
3. Pour the mixture into the lined cake tin and bake in the oven for 50–60 minutes, until golden.
4. Allow to cool in the tin for 15 minutes, then transfer to a wire rack.

SARAH WILLES

Honey cake, p.96

Sticky banana bread

Perfect for tea, perfect for elevenses, perfect toasted for breakfast with a spoon of mascarpone.

Serves 6   Preparation time: 15 minutes   Cooking time: 45 minutes

- 450g ripe bananas/3 large bananas
- 115g butter
- 170g light brown sugar
- 2 eggs
- pinch salt
- 200g plain flour
- 1 tbsp honey + 2 tsp of honey for drizzling
- ½ tsp mixed spice
- ½ tsp baking powder
- 50g sultanas

1. Preheat the oven to 150°C/gas mark 2. Grease a loaf tin and line with baking paper.
2. Mash up most of the banana, reserving enough to slice along the top of the cake.
3. In a large bowl cream together the butter and sugar until light.
4. Whisk in the eggs, followed by the mashed bananas, salt, flour, honey, mixed spice, baking powder and sultanas. Mix well.
5. Pour the mixture into the tin and slice the remaining banana in a layer across the top of the cake. Drizzle 2 tsp of honey over the top of the cake to glaze it as it cooks.
6. Place in the oven and bake for about 45 minutes, or until golden on top and cooked all the way through. Leave to cool in the tin for 15 minutes before turning onto a wire rack.

Helpful Hints:

❖ Although this cake works best in a loaf tin, you can use a round cake tin.

EMMA TINNE

Date and coconut bars

Bridget Gladwin is, in Sarah's opinion, one of the best cooks around. She single-handedly runs Nutbourne Vineyard in West Sussex, where she produces award-winning still and sparkling wines, but she always seems to have time for culinary creations, and this is one of them. Perfect as a mid afternoon pick-me-up for weary holiday makers.

Makes: 12–16 small squares   Preparation time: 10 minutes   Cooking time: 30 minutes

- 110g salted butter
- 1 heaped tbsp golden syrup
- 1 large egg, beaten
- 140g finely chopped pitted dates
- 80g demerara sugar
- 85g desiccated coconut
- 110g self-raising flour
- splash of lemon juice, to taste

1. Preheat the oven to 160°C/gas mark 3, and line a 20cm square baking tin.
2. Melt the butter and syrup together in a pan over a low heat, set aside and allow to cool for 5 minutes.
3. Add the egg, dates, sugar, coconut, flour and lemon juice to the pan with the melted butter and syrup, and stir well.
4. Pour the mixture into the lined baking tin, and press down evenly. Bake in the preheated oven for 30 minutes, or until risen and golden brown. The cake should be soft in the centre.
5. Allow the cake to cool and set a little before turning out and slicing into squares.

Helpful Hints:

❖ If your dates are very hard, it may help to soak them in boiling water for ten minutes before chopping them up. Be very careful chopping dates in your food processor if they are hard, as they can damage the blades.
❖ Double up the recipe – these bars store well in a tin. But they won't last long as they are so delicious.

BRIDGET GLADWIN

The best sticky gooey gingerbread ever

This is loved by all ages, and is a winner on cold winter shoots, picnics, after a long days skiing and with a huge cup of tea.

Serves 6   Preparation time: 10 minutes   Cooking time: 40 minutes

- 225g black treacle
- 225g butter
- 340g caster sugar
- 225g golden syrup
- 340g plain flour
- 1 tsp ground ginger
- 1 tsp mixed spice
- 170ml boiling water
- 2 eggs
- 1 tsp bicarbonate of soda

1. Preheat the oven to 180°C/gas mark 4.
2. Line a medium-sized deep baking tray, approximately 30cm squared, with greaseproof paper.
3. Melt the treacle, butter, sugar and syrup in a large saucepan. Bring to the boil and then add the flour, ginger and mixed spice. Stir well using a whisk.
4. Add the boiling water, whisk until smooth, and whisk in the egg.
5. Finally add the bicarbonate of soda, and stir well.
6. Pour into the lined baking tray and cook for 40 minutes, or until firm.
7. Leave the gingerbread to cool, then cut into squares. This is best eaten while it is still warm.

SOPHIE HEWLETT

Kirsty's extra squidgy chocolate cake

This cake is so rich and chocolatey, it requires no icing. A perfect way to use up any breadcrumbs or slices of bread you might have left from lunch.

Serves 8–10   Preparation time: 15 minutes   Cooking time: 30–40 minutes

- 250g butter
- 250g granulated sugar
- 5 eggs
- 250g ground hazelnuts, pecans or almonds
- 125g fresh breadcrumbs
- 250g plain chocolate, melted

1. Preheat the oven to 190°C/gas mark 5.
2. Grease a 20cm loose-bottomed cake tin with butter, and line with baking paper.
3. Beat together the butter and sugar in a food processor until light and fluffy. Beat in the eggs one at a time, along with a handful of the ground nuts (this prevents the mixture from curdling).
4. Fold in the remaining nuts, breadcrumbs and melted chocolate.
5. Pour the mixture into the lined cake tin and bake on the medium shelf of the oven for 30–40 minutes, or until firm. You can check it is cooked properly by inserting a skewer – it should come out clean if the cake is cooked.
6. Allow the cake to cool in the tin before turning out carefully onto a plate.

KIRSTEN MACDONALD

Buckwheat cake

Adapted from Anna Del Conte's recipe in The Classic Food of Northern Italy, *Pavillion Books, 2004, this is a perfect cake for those who are gluten intolerant, or simply like the nuttiness of buckwheat.*

Serves 6   Preparation time: 15 minutes   Cooking time: 40 minutes

- 180g fine buckwheat flour
- 3 tsp baking powder
- 1 tsp ground cinnamon
- 180g ground almonds
- zest of 1 orange
- 180g caster sugar
- 180g butter, softened
- 6 free-range eggs, separated
- 360g damson or blackberry jam
- 240g mascarpone

1. Preheat the oven to 180°C/gas mark 4.
2. Butter a 24cm loose-bottomed spring-form cake tin and line the bottom with baking parchment.
3. Sift the buckwheat flour, baking powder and cinnamon together, then stir in the ground almonds and the orange zest.
4. Beat 6 tablespoons of the sugar with the softened butter until light and creamy. Then beat in the egg yolks one by one.
5. Put the egg whites in a large and scrupulously clean bowl and whisk until soft peaks form. Start whisking in the rest of the sugar, one tablespoon at a time, whisking well after each addition until stiff and glossy.
6. Now fold in alternate spoonfuls of the buckwheat–almond mixture and the meringue into the creamed butter until well mixed.
7. Spoon the cake mixture into the buttered cake tin and bake for about 40 minutes.
8. Let the cake stand for 5 minutes before unmoulding and leave to cool.
9. With a serrated knife cut the cake in half horizontally to make two rounds, holding your hand firmly on the top cake to guide the knife.
10. Spread the jam over the bottom of the cake and the mascarpone over the top half. Sandwich the two halves together, pressing down lightly, and finish with a dusting of icing sugar.

SARAH WILLES

Rhubarb crumble cake

Serves 6 Preparation: 25 minutes Cooking time: 1 hour

- 400g rhubarb
- 3 tbsp soft brown sugar
- 2 tbsp of orange juice
- 170g softened butter
- 150g ground almonds
- 170g caster sugar
- 170g self-raising flour
- 2 tbsp ground cinnamon
- 1 tbsp ground mixed spice
- zest of 1 orange
- 2 eggs
- 100g plain flour
- 75g soft brown sugar
- 75g butter
- pinch of salt

1. Preheat the oven to 180°C/gas mark 4.
2. Wash the rhubarb well and cut into 5cm lengths. Simmer with the brown sugar and orange juice in a covered pan for 5 minutes until soft. Stir well and set aside.
3. Lightly butter a 23cm loose-bottomed spring-form tin.
4. Place the butter, ground almonds, sugar, flour, 1 teaspoon of cinnamon, mixed spice, orange zest and eggs in a food processor and mix until thick and creamy.
5. Pour the cake mixture into the tin. Drain off the rhubarb juices and gently place the rhubarb over the top of the cake mixture.
6. To make the crumble topping, mix together the plain flour, sugar, butter, the last teaspoon of cinnamon and salt. Rub the ingredients together with your fingers until resembles fine breadcrumbs. Cover the rhubarb mixture with the crumble.
7. Set the tin on a baking sheet and bake on a rack set just below the middle of the oven for 1 hour. If the cake is browning too quickly after half an hour, place some foil loosely over the top and around the sides.
8. Cool in the tin for 15 minutes before transferring to a serving plate.

Helpful Hints:

❖ **You can either warm the cake as a pudding with cream or ice cream, or eat it cold as a cake.**

BRIDGET GLADWIN

Salad suggestions – much more than just leaves …

Create some simple salads for lunch using what's in your fridge and dress at the last minute with your jar of pre-made vinaigrette. Some foods definitely work well together, others certainly don't. Here is our rough guide to successful, and unsuccessful, combinations:

Combinations that DO work in our opinion:

- Smoked chicken, hazelnuts and mango/peaches
- Parma ham, mozzarella, mint and figs/peaches/melon
- Blue cheese, pears, walnuts and endive
- Beetroot, goat's cheese and parsley
- Roasted vegetables and toasted pine nuts (omit the vinaigrette)
- Grated cabbage, carrot, toasted coriander seeds and cumin seeds
- Cooked green beans/leeks/broccoli mixed with crispy bacon and chopped boiled eggs
- Fresh tuna, tomatoes, green beans, boiled eggs, anchovies and lettuce
- Cooked chicken, croutons and cos lettuce
- Pasta, peppers, pine nuts, pesto and tomatoes
- Celery, apple, watercress and hard cheese
- Couscous, grated lemon or lime zest and chopped herbs
- Fennel, orange and basil
- Fennel, pear and pomegranate
- Green beans and toasted hazelnuts
- Chargrilled courgette ribbons with lemon juice, olive oil, feta and oregano/mint
- Sliced cucumber, dill and cider vinegar
- Toasted pitta bread, tomatoes, shredded romaine lettuce, sumac, radishes, cucumber and lemon juice
- Kalamata olives, red onion, cucumber, tomato, feta/white cheese and thyme
- Liberally use any edible flowers you can lay your hands on, such as rocket flowers, courgette flowers, chive flowers, nasturtiums and marigolds.
- If you have lovely lettuces and green leaves, keep the salad green and make a separate tomato salad

Combinations that DO NOT work in our opinion:

- Beetroot and tomato together
- Tomatoes and any fruit
- Tuna and any fruit
- Cooked mushrooms in salad
- Seeds and roasted vegetables

Marinades

While a quality piece of fresh fish or meat often needs nothing more than a sprinkle of salt and pepper, a good marinade can transform our food and tantalise our tastebuds. Dig around in your cupboards for ingredients, chop down some herbs in the garden, or follow our suggestions for the perfect marinade, and then cook in the oven, on a barbecue or over a camp fire on the beach ...

Arm yourself with a large mixing bowl, and simply combine:

Smoked paprika and lemon – perfect for pork and chicken
1 tbsp smoked paprika, juice and zest of 2 lemons, 2 tbsp olive oil, 2 sprigs rosemary, 2 cloves of garlic

Spicy Asian marinade – fish, chicken, beef, pork and lamb
1 tbsp sesame oil, 1 large red chilli, 1 knob of ginger about 10cm, zest and juice of 2 limes, 4 tbsp soy sauce, 1 tbsp fish sauce, 2 tbsp honey

Cinnamon and pomegranate molasses – chicken
1 tsp ground cinnamon, 2 tbsp pomegranate molasses, 1 tbsp olive oil, salt and pepper

Greek yoghurt, lemon and rosemary – lamb and chicken
200g approx of Greek yoghurt, 1 large knob of ginger thinly sliced, 2 lemons paired and juiced, 3 large sprigs of rosemary, 2 tbsp Dijon mustard, 5 cloves of garlic smashed

Marinade for rib-eye steaks or whole joints
200g soft brown sugar, 200ml vegetable oil, 120ml of soy sauce, 75ml red wine vinegar, 100ml fresh lemon juice, 75ml Worcestershire sauce, 2 cloves of finely chopped garlic, 1 finely sliced onion, freshly ground black pepper

If you have time, caramelise the onions from the marinade in a small pan, add the rest of the marinade, reduce and serve as a sauce with the beef.

HANDY HINTS:
* Try to marinade your fish or meat for at least 3 hours in the fridge. The longer the better.
* If your marinade contains sugar, honey or molasses, keep the heat low to avoid burning.

EMMA TINNE AND ALISON RAVENSCROFT

Aubergine and feta dip, p.107
Lyn Wood's wasabi pea dip, p.109
Beetroot andd horseradish dip, p.108

Aubergine and feta dip

This dip also goes really well with barbecued lamb.

Makes one medium-sized bowl of dip   Preparation time: 10 minutes
Cooking time: 45 minutes

- 2 aubergines
- 150g feta cheese
- 100ml olive oil
- squeeze of lemon
- 1 tbsp chopped parsley
- sea salt and black pepper

1. Preheat the oven to 220°C/gas mark 7.
2. Roast the whole aubergines on a baking tray for 45 minutes until the skin is wrinkled and the flesh is completely soft and coming away.
3. Put the aubergines in a bowl and cover with cling film. Leave to cool slightly.
4. Take the aubergines out, peel the skin off and place in a food processor with the feta.
5. Whizz until smooth, then slowly add the olive oil, followed by the salt and pepper and a squeeze of lemon.
6. Serve in a bowl topped with chopped parsley or extra crumbled feta.

DAVINA MULFORD

Beetroot and horseradish dip

Makes a small bowl of dip   Preparation time: 5 minutes

- 50g cooked and peeled beetroot
- 100g cream cheese
- 3 heaped tsp horseradish sauce
- squeeze of lemon juice
- sea salt and black pepper

1. Put the beetroot, cream cheese, horseradish sauce and lemon juice into a food processor, or use a hand-held blender. Blend the ingredients until as smooth as possible. Season with salt and pepper to taste, and add a little more lemon juice if desired.
2. Decant into a bowl and place in the fridge.
3. Scatter over toasted flaked almonds if you like, and serve with toasted pitta bread and carrot sticks.

HATTIE DEARDS

Lyn Wood's wasabi pea dip

*Fresh-tasting and unusual – perfect with cheese biscuits.
Lyn is a key volunteer and supporter of Blues in schools.*

Makes a medium-sized bowl of dip   Preparation time: 5–10 minutes
Cooling time: 30 minutes

- 175g peas, fresh or frozen
- 200g crème fraiche
- 50g cream cheese
- 1 tbsp wasabi paste (to taste)
- 1 small red chilli, deseeded and chopped (optional)
- sea salt

1. Cook the peas in boiling water for 2 to 3 minutes, and drain.
2. Add the peas, crème fraiche, cream cheese and wasabi paste to a food processor or use a hand-held blender. Blend the ingredients together until smooth. Taste and season with sea salt.
3. Spoon the dip into a bowl, mix in the chopped chilli and refrigerate until needed.

LYN WOOD

Butters

Flavoured butters are quick and easy to make, and a good way to add flavour to anything from grilled fish to baked apples. Whizz up the butter and whatever flavourings you are using (you will have to use your common sense a bit with quantities) in a food processor, spoon on to some cling film, shape into a roll and then wrap. Keep in the fridge or freezer and slice off pieces as and when you need to.

Here are some of our favourites....

Lemon zest, garlic and thyme ... lamb chops, chicken

Hazelnut and coriander ... fish, such as skate, and chicken

Basil and sun-dried tomato ... chicken and fish

Garlic and parsley ... chicken and steaks

Coriander, ginger and chilli ... fish, especially trout

Anchovy ... fish, especially brill

Dill ... salmon and vegetables

Cinnamon and walnuts ... baked apples or toasted banana bread

Sticky banana bread, p.98
Dried fruit salad, p.112

Breakfast can be the best meal of the day ...

Breakfast doesn't have to be a bowl of cereal and a slice of toast every day. Embark on another day of holidaying with a full stomach and everyone will be as happy as can be. Try one or all of the following:

- Toast a slice of banana bread or panettone, and serve with a spoon of mascarpone.
- Toast a couple of potato farls. Spread them with butter and top with a couple of large grilled field mushrooms and season with Worcestershire sauce.
- Puree a punnet of ripe strawberries, and stir into a bowl of Greek yoghurt.
- If you are feeling Mediterranean, make pan boli. Toast sour dough or any country-style bread. Rub the toasted bread with a clove of peeled garlic, drizzle with olive oil and vigorously rub over half a very ripe tomato. Season with black pepper and sea salt.
- Scramble eggs until only just done, and serve with serrano ham, or good quality parma ham.
- For a hearty start to the day serve fresh bagels with pastrami and thinly sliced gherkins.
- Make a large platter of pineapple, paw-paw and melon. Cut them all into large wedges, which makes them easy for children to eat with their hands.
- Toast some soda bread, spread with butter and serve with smoked salmon and a squeeze of lemon juice.
- Dried fruit salad – enjoy this old classic for breakfast with some natural yoghurt. It will keep in the fridge for a few days: *500g dried fruit (apricots, figs and prunes); 600ml fresh orange juice; 3 tbsp fruit sugar or caster sugar; 2 apples, cored and cut into 8 pieces each; 1 handful sultanas; 2 sliced bananas. Simmer the dried fruit, orange juice and sugar in a pan for 20 minutes, until relatively soft. Add the apple and continue to simmer for another 10 minutes. Remove from the heat, add the sultanas and sliced bananas. Vary the fruit if you prefer other dried fruits instead.*

Sweetcorn fritters
with roasted tomatoes and bacon

Don't be put off by the seemingly long list of ingredients – these are really quick to rustle up, and a breakfast not to be forgotten.

Serves 4–6   Preparation time: 10 minutes   Cooking time: 10 minutes

- 6 tomatoes
- 1 tbsp olive oil
- 6 tbsp polenta
- 110g plain flour
- 1 tsp baking powder
- pinch dried chilli flakes
- ½ tsp thyme leaves
- 4 spring onions, finely chopped
- 250g sweetcorn kernels (fresh or canned)
- 2 eggs, beaten
- 200ml milk
- 2 tbsp melted butter
- 3 tbsp sunflower oil
- 12 slices smoked streaky bacon
- 250ml pot of crème fraiche
- sea salt and black pepper

1. Preheat oven to 180°C/gas mark 4.
2. Slice tomatoes in half, drizzle with olive oil, season with salt and pepper, and roast in the oven for 15–20 minutes.
3. To make the sweetcorn cakes, combine the polenta, flour, baking powder, chilli flakes and thyme in a bowl. Add the spring onions, sweetcorn, beaten eggs, milk and melted butter, and stir well until you have a batter.
4. Heat the sunflower oil in a frying pan and drop tablespoons of the sweetcorn mixture in to the pan. Cook for about 2 minutes on each side until golden brown. Drain on kitchen paper and keep warm.
5. Meanwhile grill the bacon on both sides, and remove the tomatoes from the oven.
6. Serve 2 sweetcorn fritters per person, and top with crème fraiche, tomatoes and bacon.

DAVINA MULFORD

Huevos Rancheros

Fiona Beckett's mighty Mexican-style egg breakfast taken from Beyond Baked Beans, Absolute Press, 2004, is the perfect feast for holiday makers who are heading out for a busy day, or for those who are horribly hungover.

Serves 4   Preparation time: 5 minutes   Cooking time: 15–20 minutes

- 6 tbsp sunflower or olive oil
- 1 large onion, roughly chopped
- 2 green chillis, or ½ tsp chilli powder/cayenne pepper
- 2 cloves garlic, roughly chopped
- 1 tin of chopped tomatoes, or 6 very ripe tomatoes
- 1 tbsp chopped coriander or parsley
- 4–8 corn tortillas, dependent on how many each person wants
- 4–8 eggs, dependent on how many each person wants

1. Heat 3 tablespoons of oil in a medium pan, add the chopped onion, chilli, garlic and tomatoes. Cook for about 5–10 minutes, stirring occasionally, until most of the tomato juice has evaporated and it is starting to go jammy.
2. Season with salt and add the coriander or parsley. Tip the contents into a bowl and set aside.
3. Using a kitchen towel wipe clean the pan, add 1 tablespoon of the remaining oil and swirl it around. Warm each of the corn tortillas in the pan, one by one, pressing down on each side for 30 seconds.
4. While you are warming through the tortillas, add the remaining 2 tablespoons of oil to a non-stick frying pan. Heat through, and fry the eggs until cooked to your liking.
5. Place the eggs on top of each tortilla, and spoon the hot salsa onto the whites of the eggs, leaving the yolks showing.

FIONA BECKETT

Index of recipes